Kickoff English Mystery
「キックオフ ミステリー」― 楽しく学べる総合英語

Terry O'Brien
Kei Mihara
Akinori Usami
Hiroshi Kimura

NAN'UN-DO

Kickoff English Mystery

Copyright© 2019

by
Terry O'Brien
Kei Mihara
Akinori Usami
Hiroshi Kimura

All Rights Reserved
No part of this book may be reproduced in any form without written permission from the authors and Nan'un-do Co., Ltd.

このテキストの音声を無料で視聴（ストリーミング）・ダウンロードできます。自習用音声としてご活用ください。
以下のサイトにアクセスしてテキスト番号で検索してください。

https://nanun-do.com　テキスト番号 [**511954**]

※ 無線 LAN（WiFi）に接続してのご利用を推奨いたします。
※ 音声ダウンロードは Zip ファイルでの提供になります。
　お使いの機器によっては別途ソフトウェア（アプリケーション）の導入が必要となります。

Kickoff English Mystery 音声ダウンロードページは
左記の QR コードからもご利用になれます。

Read by
Emma Howard
Michael Rhys

はじめに

本書は自ら進んで読み、学びたくなるテキストです。不思議で謎めいたミステリーは、いつの時代も人々の知的好奇心を掻き立てます。ミステリーを味わい、謎解きを楽しみながら、知らず知らずのうちに英文に没頭している自分に気づくでしょう。

本書は各ユニットのリーディングのミステリー・ストーリーをコアにして展開します。まず自動車事故を発端に「謎」が配置されます。テレビのニュース速報は、ある若い女性がノースフィールドで車にはねられ病院に運ばれたと伝えます。これは事故なのか、事件なのか、次々と示される「手がかり」をもとに、警察はどのように「謎」を解いていくでしょうか。読み手は面白いストーリーに、次第に引き込まれていきます。そして驚愕のクライマックスで「謎」が解き明かされます。

本書は英語の語彙や表現を「覚える」だけでなく、「考える」英語力を養うことを指針としています。効果的に配置された練習問題を解くことで、リーディング、ライティング、リスニングの力が身につくように構成されています。つまり、英語の基礎をしっかり固め、「考える」英語力を強化することを目的とした、初級・中級レベルの英語総合教材です。

本書は学生が自ら考え、判断し、問題を解決する思考力を養うことができるような形式にしています。主体的に学習できるように多彩な練習問題を盛り込み、楽しく無理なく英語に向き合っていただけるのが特長です。

本書の特長

1. 220-280 語程度の英文を読むことでリーディング力を強化
2. 語彙の意味、T/F 問題、応答問題で、本文の内容理解度を確認
3. 60 語程度の会話文で、3 人の会話や図表などを含む問題を解き、リスニング力をアップ
4. 80 語程度の TOEIC 形式の文法問題でリーディングの基本的な表現力を補強
5. 英文を完成することでライティング力を習得
6. イラストを説明する 80 語程度の英文中の語彙を考えることで語彙力を定着

本書を使った主体的な学習によって、ミステリーを楽しみつつ、「考える」英語力を確実にマスターしてくださることを願っています。

2019 年 1 月　著者

本書の使い方

全体で 15 ユニットです。各ユニットはリーディング、ライティング、リスニングで構成しています。リーディングでは内容理解度を確認するために 3 つのパターンの練習問題、TOEIC 形式の長文空所補充問題があります。ライティングでは 3 つのパターンの練習問題、イラスト描写問題があります。リスニングでは写真描写問題、会話文の完成や応答問題があります。

Warm-up
CD を聞いて空所に単語を書き、写真を適切に描写しているものを (A) (B) から選んでください。

1 Reading
＜主な登場人物＞
テッド・ブライソン：BEC 社の経営者で技術者
ソニア：コンサルタント会社の女性社長
ボブ・カッスルフォード：タクシードライバー
リリー・バターカップ：テッドのオフィスの向かいに住んでいる人
ビリー：ソニアの会社のドライバー

Exercises
Ⓐ Vocabulary
本文中の単語について、その意味に合う語句を a 〜 e から 1 つ選んでください。

Ⓑ True or False
適切なボールド体の語句を選んで英文を完成してください。次にその英文が本文の内容に合っていれば T (True)、間違っていれば F (False) を選んでください。

Ⓒ Choosing
本文の内容について、質問に対する適切な答えを (A) (B) から選んでください。

2 Conversation
Ⓐ Q&A
まず会話を聞いてください。次に質問文の空所に単語を書き、適切な答えを (A) 〜 (C) から選んでください。
＊前のトラックが会話、後ろのトラックが質問文です。

Ⓑ L&F
もう一度会話を聞いて空所に単語を書き、会話を完成してください。

3 Text Completion
長文を完成するため、空所に入る適切な表現を (A) 〜 (D) から 1 つ選んでください。

4 Writing
Ⓐ 指示に従って英文を完成してください。
Ⓑ 空所内の語句を並べ替えてください。
Ⓒ 空所に単語を書いて英文を完成してください。

5 Look and Write
イラストの説明になるように空所に入る単語を語群より選び、必要なら適切な形に変えて書いてください。

Grammar Check
各ユニットで扱われる文法事項を確認してください。

Contents

Unit 1 An Accident   present tense / past tense   6
車にはねられた若い女性の謎

Unit 2 Did You See Anything?   there is / are   11
ひき逃げ事件を目撃した人は地元の警察に！

Unit 3 The Bryson Engineering Company   articles / pronouns   16
エンジンデザインで有名なテッドの会社

Unit 4 An Interview   nouns: countable / uncountable   21
女性インタビュアーの不可解な振る舞い

Unit 5 The Police Are Puzzled.   comparisons   26
事件の真相に戸惑う警察

Unit 6 Two Witnesses   adjectives / adverbs   31
事件を語る 2 人の証言

Unit 7 The Car Driver   future / present perfect   36
車で送迎を頼まれたドライバー

Unit 8 Office Security   passive voice / causative   41
テッドのオフィス・セキュリティー対策は？

Unit 9 Her Memory Is Coming Back!   direct speech / reported speech   46
徐々に回復する女性の意識

Unit 10 Is Ted Bryson a Criminal?   progressives / auxiliary verbs   51
テッドは犯罪者なのか？

Unit 11 Who Is She?   infinitives / gerunds   56
女性は会社経営者なのか、その正体は？

Unit 12 Do You Realise Who You Are?   prepositions / conjunctions   61
必要とされる監視システム

Unit 13 How Are You?   imperatives / exclamations   66
医者も驚くほどの回復力

Unit 14 A Face in the Crowd   relatives   71
車椅子で病院から謎の失踪

Unit 15 Did You Watch TV Last Night?   subjunctives   76
国際会議場に謎の女性の姿が！

Unit 1 An Accident   present tense / past tense

Warm-up

Listen and fill in the blanks with the words. Then choose the statement (A) or (B) that describes what you see in the picture.

(A) The front of the car is (   ).

(B) The four men are (   ) on the pavement.

Answer (   )

1 Reading

Read the passage below and then do the exercises that follow.

　Good morning, and welcome to News at 7. It is a nice warm morning out there, with not a cloud in the sky—a perfect day for a holiday. But unfortunately, most of us have to go to work.
　We will look at the weather in more detail a little later, but first let's catch up on the latest news. Our main story this morning concerns a hit-and-run accident that took place in Northfield at around 8:00 p.m. last night. A young woman pedestrian was hit in a crosswalk by a vehicle travelling at a high speed. The vehicle did not stop— the driver simply drove off. The impact was so great that the victim flew up over the pavement and into a car park, nearly 10 metres away. A neighbour heard something, ran out, and found the badly injured young woman lying on the ground and not moving.
　An ambulance rushed the victim to St Mary's Hospital. She had hit her head and was unconscious and also had a broken leg and arm. The woman had no ID, so her identity remains a mystery. She is still unconscious, but with treatment, she should wake up and be able to speak in a few days. Doctors say she is lucky to be alive.

> **Notes** out there「外は」　in more detail「より詳しく」　catch up on「～を伝える」　hit-and-run 「ひき逃げ」　take place「起こる」

Exercises

A Vocabulary

Match the words on the left with their meanings (a-e) on the right. Write the letters of each meaning on the lines.

1. concern   _____
2. impact   _____
3. pedestrian   _____
4. treatment   _____
5. unconscious   _____

a. a person who is walking along a street or road
b. a way of dealing with a disease or injury
c. force; collision
d. in a deep sleep
e. to relate or belong to

B True or False

Choose the word in bold that correctly completes each sentence. Then, based on the information in the reading passage, circle T if the sentence is true or F if it is false.

1. The (**injure** / **injured**) woman is quite old. T F
2. The neighbour (**driven** / **drove**) the woman to the hospital. T F
3. The woman will (**is** / **be**) able to speak in a few days. T F

C Choosing

Choose the correct answer (A) or (B) for each question below.

1. Why can't all the people listening to the news enjoy the good weather?
   (A) It is going to rain.   (B) They have to go to work.

2. How was the woman badly injured?
   (A) She slipped and fell on the pavement.   (B) She was hit by a fast-moving car.

3. Why was she lucky?
   (A) She wasn't killed.   (B) The driver of the car was a doctor.

2 Conversation

A Q&A

 04   05

Listen to the conversation. Then listen to each question and fill in the blanks, and choose the best answer.

1. Where is the _____ _____ now?
   (A) She is at home.   (B) She is in the ambulance.   (C) She is in hospital.

2. Where did they _____ _____ ?
   (A) In a car park   (B) In a car   (C) On the road

3. Why is _____ _____ a mystery?
   (A) The vehicle was travelling too fast.   (B) No one knows who the woman is.
   (C) There were no witnesses.

B L&F

Now, as you listen to the conversation again, fill in the blanks.

man: There's something strange on the TV news.
woman: What do you 1( ) by "strange"?
man: A young woman is in hospital. She was badly 2( ).
woman: So, who is she? Where does she come 3( )?
man: Well, that's the mystery. Nobody 4( ) the answer.
woman: Where did all this happen?
man: A neighbour 5( ) her lying and not moving in a car park in Northfield. It looks like a hit-and-run.

3 Text Completion

Select the best choice for each numbered blank in the text below.

It's getting worse. Every morning the news ------- about yet another crash, where
1.
the driver doesn't stop. Parents used to teach their kids to respect others. If
parents couldn't ------- that, teachers would try. But today, parents and teachers
2.
are not allowed to shout at kids, which is why I think we have so many hit-and-run
accidents. A car is like a "black magic" box. Once a person ------- behind the wheel,
3.
the person changes into an aggressive and dangerous driver. -------
4.

1. (A) are
   (B) is
   (C) was
   (D) were

2. (A) be
   (B) did
   (C) do
   (D) does

3. (A) drive
   (B) gets
   (C) holds
   (D) kept

4. (A) All young people are the same.
   (B) Enjoy life while you are young.
   (C) Driving fast is great fun.
   (D) We have to do something about this.

4 Writing

A Rewrite each sentence below according to the instructions.

1. The cause of the crash is still under investigation. (疑問文に)
   _____

2. The driver pulls over after hitting the woman. (過去時制の否定文に)
   _____

3. The ambulance took her <u>to the hospital</u>. (下線部を問う疑問文に)
   _____

B Rearrange the words in the parentheses to make correct sentences.

4. なぜドライバーが左によけたのか明らかではありません。
   It is (clear / not / swerved / the driver / why) to the left.
   _____

5. その女性は道路を横切っているときに大ケガをしました。
   The woman was (crossing / injured / seriously / the road / while).
   _____

6. ケガをしている人がいたら、できるだけ早く救急車を呼んでください。
   If someone is injured, (an ambulance / as / as / call / soon) possible.
   _____

C Fill in the missing words to complete each sentence.

7. 救急車が事故現場に着くのに10分かかりました。
   It took 10 (   ) for the ambulance to (   ) at the crash (   ).

8. 優れた治療のおかげで、その女性はケガから早く回復しています。
   Thanks to excellent (   ), the woman is (   ) a quick (   ) (   ) her injuries.

5 Look and Write

As you look at the illustration below, fill in the blanks in the paragraph that follows with words from the box. Change the word's form where necessary.

| hit | land | keep | know | shock | were |

I saw this on the TV this morning, and I was ₁(   ). The announcer said that a young woman was ₂(   ) by a car or maybe a truck that was going very fast. Acccording to the police, she flew ten metres and ₃(   ) in a car park. They say that the driver didn't stop. The driver just ₄(   ) going. The doctors at the hospital ₅(   ) surprised that the woman didn't die. The saddest thing about all this is that nobody ₆(   ) who she is.

Grammar Check

現在形

1. 現在の動作・状態

James works hard most of the time. （ジェームズはほとんどの時間、懸命に働きます）
Karen lives in Liverpool. （カレンはリバプールに住んでいます）
I like to read mystery novels. （ミステリー小説を読むのが好きです）

2. 一般的な事実、ことわざ

Water consists of hydrogen and oxygen. （水は水素と酸素から成っています）
There is no royal road to learning. （学問に王道なし）

過去形

1. 過去の動作・状態

Robert worked hard every day. （ロバートは毎日懸命に働きました）
Marie lived in Australia. （マリーはオーストラリアに住んでいました）
I thought that he was sincere. （私は彼が誠実だと思いました）

2. 過去の反復動作

I went to school by bike in those days. （当時は、自転車で通学しました）

Unit 2 Did You See Anything?

there is / are

Warm-up

Listen and fill in the blanks with the words. Then choose the statement (A) or (B) that describes what you see in the picture.

(A) All the women are (   ) their hands.

(B) Most of the women are (   ) upward.

Answer (   )

1 Reading

Read the passage below and then do the exercises that follow.

Good morning to all our viewers. For the second day in a row, it's a beautiful day out there. Our forecasters say this fine, warm weather will remain with us until late afternoon. So, for now at least, forget your jacket and get out and enjoy the sunshine while you can.

But now, I have a favour to ask of you. We need your help. Yesterday, we reported that a young woman had been seriously injured and she is now in hospital—on the road to recovery, thankfully. On Monday evening at around 8, she was struck by a car or possibly a small truck and knocked 10 metres away into a car park. The driver failed to stop. If you happened to see or hear anything unusual at around that time, please let us know. If you've seen a car with a damaged front end in your neighbourhood, give the police a call.

The problem is that the police cannot identify the victim. She has no ID, no mobile, no purse or driving license. And because she is unconscious, she is unable to speak and cannot tell us who she is.

The woman is about 160 cm tall, has long, dark, straight hair, and is probably in her late 20s. The police have released this sketch. If you think you may know or have met the woman, please contact the police immediately. Somewhere out there, there is a driver who not only hit an innocent pedestrian, but who also criminally drove away from the scene of the accident. We must find this person and bring him or her to justice!

Notes for the second day in a row「2日連続で」   on the road「途上にあって」   identify「身元を特定する」   scene of the accident「事故現場」   bring ... to justice「〜を裁判にかける」

Exercises

A Vocabulary

Match the words on the left with their meanings (a-e) on the right. Write the letters of the meanings on the lines.

1. viewer _____
2. favour _____
3. release _____
4. sketch _____
5. innocent _____

a. a drawing that shows the features of a person
b. a person who watches television
c. a special request
d. not having done anything bad or wrong
e. to show the public

B True or False

Choose the word in bold that correctly completes each sentence. Then, based on the information in the reading passage, circle T if the sentence is true or F if it is false.

1. Viewers don't need to (**wear** / **wearing**) warm clothing today. T F
2. The police (**doesn't** / **don't**) know who the young lady is. T F
3. A photo of the driver (**is** / **are**) being shown on TV. T F

C Choosing

Choose the correct answer (A) or (B) for each question below.

1. What is today's good news?
   (A) The fine weather will continue until tomorrow.
   (B) It's going to be nice and warm most of the day.

2. How was the young lady identified?
   (A) The police used her phone.   (B) She hasn't been identified yet.

3. What does the newscaster want people to do?
   (A) Stay tuned for more weather news
   (B) Report any information they may have about the accident

2 Conversation

A Q&A

 08   09

Listen to the conversation with three speakers. Then listen to each question and fill in the blanks, and choose the best answer.

1. Why are the _____ _____?
   (A) There are many dangerous places.
   (B) There is a dangerous driver around somewhere.
   (C) They are not feeling well.

2. What _____ _____ person do they think the driver is?
   (A) Dangerous　　　　(B) Innocent　　　　(C) Mysterious

3. Who does Karen think the _____ _____?
   (A) The driver is a man.
   (B) The driver is a woman.
   (C) To tell the truth, she doesn't know.

B L&F

Now, as you listen to the conversation again, fill in the blanks.

man: It is frightening to think that there is such a ₁(　　　) driver out there somewhere.

woman A: I wonder if his family or friends know the ₂(　　　) about him?

woman B: I ₃(　　　) not, Karen.

man: I have a question, Karen. You said "his" and "him". How do you ₄(　　　) that the driver is a man?

woman A: Well, I ₅(　　　) know who the driver is. The driver might be a man or a woman.

3 Text Completion

Select the best choice for each numbered blank in the text below.

There ------- an old woman who lives near me. Every morning she gets up early
　　　　1.
and ------- the road and storm drains outside her house. That's good of her, but she
　　2.
does this work at daybreak, before most people ------- up. When I moved into my
　　　　　　　　　　　　　　　　　　　　　　　3.
house, I carefully put my kitchen waste out on the correct day, but I often noticed
later that my plastic garbage bag had been opened. The old woman had been
checking to see if my garbage was the correct kind for that day. -------
　　　　　　　　　　　　　　　　　　　　　　　　　　　　　　　4.

1. (A) are
   (B) is
   (C) was
   (D) were

2. (A) clean
   (B) cleans
   (C) cleaned
   (D) cleaning

3. (A) gets
   (B) asleep
   (C) wake
   (D) awake

4. (A) I always say "Good morning" to her.
   (B) I don't usually have much garbage.
   (C) She is a nice lady, but she is too nosy.
   (D) We recycle plastic on Tuesdays.

4 Writing

A Rewrite each sentence below according to the instructions.

1. No driver was at the scene of the accident. (There で始める文に)

   _____

2. The police tried to identify the victim from her appearance. (否定文に)

   _____

3. <u>At around 8:00 p.m.</u> a woman was hit by a speeding vehicle. (下線部を問う疑問文に)

   _____

B Rearrange the words in the parentheses to make correct sentences.

4. ここでは、たくさんの重大な自動車事故があります。
   There (accidents / are / car / many / serious) here.

   _____

5. 彼女の身元は、彼女が目を覚まして警察に自分が誰であるかを言うまで不明のままでしょう。
   Her identity will remain uncertain (and tells / she / the police / until / wakes up) who she is.

   _____

6. スコットランドを旅行中に、何か面白いものを見ましたか。
   Did (anything / interesting / see / while / you) you were travelling in Scotland?

   _____

C Fill in the missing words to complete each sentence.

7. 天気は3日間連続、雨で寒いです。
   For the (   ) day in a (   ), the weather has been (   ) and cold.

8. 警察は地元の住民に、事故の被害者の身元確認をするのを手伝ってくれるように頼みました。
   The police have asked (   ) residents to (   ) them (   ) the accident (   ).

5 Look and Write

As you look at the illustration below, fill in the blanks in the paragraph that follows with words from the box. Change the word's form where necessary.

are   ask   can   if   is   neighbour

The same story was on the local news again this morning. The announcer was 1(   ) the public to help find out who this young woman is. I hope somebody 2(   ) recognise her soon. All the 3(   ) are talking about the accident, and they feel frightened that there 4(   ) such a bad person still out there driving. There 5(   ) a lot of little children who live near here, as well as many old people. 6(   ) they were hit by a speeding vehicle, they would probably not survive.

Grammar Check

There is / are 構文

1. There is [...], There are [...] の使い方
- there は形式的な主語で、[...] が意味上の主語にあたります。
- 名詞 [...] が単数形なら There is、名詞 [...] が複数形なら There are

There is a new clothing **store** near here. (この近くに新しい衣料品店があります)
There are some good **restaurants** on this street. (この通りにはいくつかの良いレストランがあります)

2. There is / are の否定文、疑問文、未来形

There are no parking lots around here. (このあたりに駐車場はありません)
Are there any questions? (ご質問はありますか)
There will be a meeting tomorrow. (明日会合があります)

3. There is の慣用表現

There is no turning back. (もう後戻りできません)
There is no use in arguing with her. (彼女と議論しても無駄です)

Unit 3 The Bryson Engineering Company articles / pronouns

Warm-up

Listen and fill in the blanks with the words. Then choose the statement (A) or (B) that describes what you see in the picture.

(A) There are some (   ) on the roof.

(B) There are (   ) on the ground and on the first floor.

Answer (   )

1 Reading

Read the passage below and then do the exercises that follow.

　Ted Bryson's company's office was old, small, and usually untidy. He employed only a dozen diligent workers, including the engineers who worked in the ancient factory behind the office. When Ted sketched out an idea for a new design on paper, his engineers changed it into the real thing. Ted's company may not have looked all
5 that impressive. But it was very efficient and well known internationally.

　Ted was an engineer himself, one of the best in the whole country. His head was filled with engineering problems and how to solve them. The success of his company came from the ideas Ted had for making one thing in particular—the complex parts that go into rocket engines. His company produced these parts slowly and carefully,
10 and, surprisingly, very cheaply. When his company succeeded in making a new part, Ted became as excited as a kid. But Ted had one big problem: other companies desperately wanted to copy his designs.

　Actually, it had never occurred to Ted that others would love to get hold of his innovative designs. He had never really thought about improving his company's
15 security. Every night, he would simply clear off his design desk and lock all his papers into an old steel office desk.

　Ah … and now Ted has just remembered that it is Friday and that he has to tidy the office a little earlier than usual. A reporter from a local newspaper is coming to interview him in the evening.

> **Notes**　**not ... all that**「それほど〜でない」　**well known**「よく知られた」　**in the whole country**「国内で」　**complex part**「複雑な部品」　**become as excited as ...**「〜と同じくらいワクワクする」　**get hold of**「〜を手に入れる」　**clear off**「片づける」

16

Exercises

A Vocabulary

Match the words on the left below with their meanings (a-e) on the right. Write the letters of each meaning on the lines.

1. untidy _____
2. ancient _____
3. copy _____
4. innovative _____
5. improve _____

a. old, having existed for a long time
b. not neat or orderly
c. using new ideas or methods
d. to make something better
e. to make something that looks just like the original

B True or False

Choose the word in bold that correctly completes each sentence. Then, based on the information in the reading passage, circle T if the sentence is true or F if it is false.

1. (**A** / **The**) workers in Ted's company are all quite old, untidy, and lazy.   T F
2. Ted is known as one of (**a** / **the**) top engineers in the country.   T F
3. Ted has just remembered that (**he** / **him**) has an appointment this evening.   T F

C Choosing

Choose the correct answer (A) or (B) for each question below.

1. Who changed Ted's ideas into the real thing?
   (A) His engineers   (B) Ted himself

2. What did other engineering businesses want?
   (A) They wanted to take Ted's workers.   (B) They wanted to get hold of Ted's designs.

3. How did Ted feel about his company's security?
   (A) He never worried about it.   (B) He had an old steel desk.

2 Conversation

A Q&A

Listen to the conversation and see the graphic. Then listen to each question and fill in the blanks, and choose the best answer.

timetable

level	# of days	completion day
1	five days	Friday
2	four days	Thursday
3	three days	Wednesday

1. _____ _____ does it take to make a very difficult design?
   (A) Five days   (B) Just one week   (C) Three working days

2. What does the customer _____ _____ company to do?
   (A) He wants them to finish it today.
   (B) He wants them to start to make the part now.
   (C) He wants to pick it up tomorrow.

3. Look at the graphic. Which of these levels is the _____ _____?
   (A) Level 1   (B) Level 2   (C) Level 3

B L&F

Now, as you listen to the conversation again, fill in the blanks.

customer: Can you make this part before the weekend?
engineer: Well, let's look at the timetable on the 1(_____) over there. If it is an easy level 3, it will 2(_____) only three days. But if it is a level 2, it will take four days. A level 1 takes five full days.
customer: I'm sure it is level 2.
engineer: Then if we start now, I think we can 3(_____) it on time by Thursday evening.
customer: Great. Could 4(_____) do that then, please? I'll come to 5(_____) it up on Friday morning.

3 Text Completion

Select the best choice for each numbered blank in the text below.

I come from a small family. There is my dad, mum and, of course, me. My dad has two sisters, Florence and Brenda. Mum has only one sister. ------- is called Susan, and so I have three aunts, but ------- uncles. Dad's dad, my grandfather, is an interesting man. He is in ------- 70s, very tall, and still a very active person. He goes out walking with his friends, almost every day, and he usually takes his camera with him. His photos of the old houses and rice fields in his neighbourhood are great. -------
4.

1. (A) She
   (B) Her
   (C) He
   (D) It

2. (A) a
   (B) an
   (C) no
   (D) the

3. (A) he
   (B) his
   (C) him
   (D) himself

4. (A) There is a rice field near her house.
   (B) When I get old, I'm going to be just like my sister.
   (C) My camera was made in Switzerland.
   (D) You would be surprised at how beautiful they are.

4 Writing

A Rewrite each sentence below according to the instructions.

1. In the morning <u>Betty</u> always cleans <u>Betty's</u> desk and office. （下線部を代名詞に代えて）

   _____

2. It occurred to <u>Ted</u> that other companies wanted to copy <u>Ted's</u> ideas.
   （下線部を代名詞に代えて否定文に）

   _____

3. Other companies desperately wanted to get hold of <u>his designs</u>. （下線部を問う疑問文に）

   _____

B Rearrange the words in the parentheses to make correct sentences.

4. 私が野球の試合でホームランを打った時、私の父は子供と同じくらいワクワクしました。
   When I hit a home run at a baseball game, (as / as / became / excited / my father) a kid.

   _____

5. その製品は過去に高品質であったにもかかわらず、もはや人気がありません。
   Despite (had / in / quality / the high / the products) the past, they are no longer popular.

   _____

6. 午後、キャロルは台所を掃除し、皿を食器棚にしまいました。
   In the afternoon Carol cleaned (and / into / put / the dishes / the kitchen) a cupboard.

   _____

C Fill in the missing words to complete each sentence.

7. 私の知っている女性は、家族の世話をするだけでなく、自分自身の会社も経営しています。
   A woman I know not only takes care of (　　　　　) family, but (　　　　　) also runs (　　　　　) own company.

8. 日本の高い国際的な評価は、勤勉さ、協調性、忍耐力を含む日本人の国民性に由来します。
   Japan's high international reputation (　　　　　) from (　　　　　) Japanese national character, which includes (　　　　　), cooperativeness, and (　　　　　).

5 Look and Write

As you look at the illustration below, fill in the blanks in the paragraph that follows with words from the box. Change the word's form where necessary.

> a   his   like   one   run   the

Ted Bryson is an interesting man. His father was an engineer, and a good 1(   ). Ted followed in 2(   ) father's footsteps and now 3(   ) the company. Ted has been very successful, and his ideas and products are now at 4(   ) top of the engineering industry in this country. You would think that Ted is 5(   ) special person. Well, just look at his desk! It looks 6(   ) anybody else's desk. You would never guess that a brilliant man makes internationally famous designs there.

Grammar Check

冠詞

1. 不定冠詞 a/ an
・初めて話題に上る、数えられる単数名詞につけます。
Do you live in a dormitory or a flat? (寮に住んでいますか、アパートに住んでいますか)
It is an ad for an exciting new restaurant. (それはワクワクするような新しいレストランの広告です)

2. 定冠詞 the
・可算・不可算、単数・複数を問わず名詞の前につき、特定のものを表します。
The woman I saw last night at the station was my boss. (昨夜駅で見かけた女性は私の上司でした)
・状況から特定性が明らかな場合
Pass me the salt, please. (塩を取ってください)
・限定形容詞の最上級
The smallest unit of matter is the atom. (物質の最小の単位は原子です)

代名詞

1. 人称代名詞：we, my, him, mine, yourself など
I live next door to my friend Brian. (私は友人ブライアンの隣に住んでいます)
Please do it yourself. (どうぞ自分でやってください)

2. 指示代名詞：this, that, these, those など
This is our new product. (これが私たちの新製品です)
The old man's movements were those of a much younger man.
(その老人の動きは、はるかに若い人の動きでした)

Unit 4 An Interview   nouns: countable / uncountable

Warm-up

Listen and fill in the blanks with the words. Then choose the statement (A) or (B) that describes what you see in the picture.

(A) They are (   ) across a table at work.

(B) They are (   ) a big meal at a restaurant.

   Answer (   )

1 Reading

Read the passage below and then do the exercises that follow.

   Ted's interview went very well. A bright young woman from *The Northfield Gazette* showed up to ask him a lot of questions about his company and his background in engineering.

   "How long have you been in this business?" she asked smiling, sitting across a table from Ted. He told her that his father had started Bryson Engineering Company thirty years ago at a time when most other engineering companies had trouble making complex rocket engine parts. "I was born into engineering," Ted said proudly. "When I was little, Dad didn't read me bedtime stories like other parents did. He used to sit on my bed and tell me how rocket engines worked and explain all the difficulties involved in making parts for them. I loved listening to him. I started here as soon as I left school. But then, a few years ago, Dad died from cancer. So I took over as director."

   The woman asked Ted if he had any photographs of his father. "I think so," Ted said. "Let me go look for them." When Ted got up and went into the next office, the woman quickly reached into her handbag. She took out two soft plastic balls—about the size of tennis balls. She then quickly made an impression of two keys that were lying on the table. One was for Ted's office door. The other fitted into the lock on Ted's old steel desk—where he kept his papers. The reporter's heart was beating fast. She hoped that she would not start sweating.

   When Ted returned with some old newspaper photos, he didn't notice a thing.

Notes   *The Northfield Gazette*「ノースフィールド・ガゼット新聞」   be born into「～に生まれる」   bedtime story「寝る前のお話」   take over「引き継ぐ」   plastic ball「プラスチック型取り粘土」   make an impression of「～の型を取る」

Exercises

A Vocabulary

Match the words on the left below with their meanings (a-e) on the right. Write the letters of each meaning on the lines.

1. background _____
2. cancer _____
3. director _____
4. fit _____
5. beat _____

a. a person who controls a company
b. a serious disease
c. the social position that a person comes from
d. to be the right size for something
e. to hit or pound repeatedly

B True or False

Choose the word in bold that correctly completes each sentence. Then, based on the information in the reading passage, circle T if the sentence is true or F if it is false.

1. Ted has had an (**interest** / **interesting**) in engineering since he was little.   T F
2. When his father died, Ted became the company's (**boss** / **bosses**).   T F
3. The reporter asked Ted to make (**copy** / **copies**) of two of his keys.   T F

C Choosing

Choose the correct answer (A) or (B) for each question below.

1. What did the reporter want to know?
   (A) About Ted's mother   (B) About Ted's company's history

2. When did Ted become interested in engineering?
   (A) Only recently   (B) He was born into it.

3. What unusual thing did she do when Ted wasn't looking?
   (A) She copied his keys.   (B) She looked at some old photos.

2 Conversation

A Q&A

Listen to the conversation. Then listen to each question and fill in the blanks, and choose the best answer.

1. _____ _____ Ted begin the conversation?
   (A) He asked her name.   (B) He showed her where to sit.
   (C) He gave her one of his business cards.

2. Why did Ted become _____ _____?
   (A) He became interested in it while at school.
   (B) He was born into it.
   (C) There was no other work in those days.

3. What did Ted imply about _____ _____ ?
   (A) His kids are pleased to have such a famous father.
   (B) His wife is helping out with the family business.
   (C) They are unhappy because they don't see much of him.

B L&F

Now, as you listen to the conversation again, fill in the blanks.

Ted: Please, sit over here, at this table. Sorry for the mess. Now, what would you ₁( ) to know?
reporter: First of all, why did you become an engineer?
Ted: I just followed in my father's ₂( ). He started this company.
reporter: I know you work very hard, but do you have any free ₃( ) to enjoy yourself?
Ted: Not much. Just one day a week, Sunday. It is a big ₄( ) on my family.
reporter: Well, thank you for being ₅( ), Mr Bryson.

3 Text Completion

Select the best choice for each numbered blank in the text below.

reporter: You seem to be on the ---₁--- from morning to night. How do you do it?
Peter: I make sure I get enough sleep. I need at least seven hours. Then I am careful about what I eat. I usually have ---₂---, an egg, and some fruit — something like a banana or half an apple. I'm very busy at work, so I don't often have time to do any ---₃--- in the gym. But I don't worry too much about that, because there is always another day. ---₄---

1. (A) boring
   (B) busy
   (C) go
   (D) out

2. (A) a bread
   (B) some bread
   (C) some breads
   (D) a slice of breads

3. (A) train
   (B) trainer
   (C) trainee
   (D) training

4. (A) Actually, I like my busy days.
   (B) Stress can make you physically ill.
   (C) I'm feeling stressed a lot.
   (D) I'm afraid I'm only free on Sundays.

4 Writing

A Rewrite each sentence below according to the instructions.

1. This young man took over the company as the CEO. （疑問文に）

2. The police asked the <u>man</u> if he had any money in his pockets. （man を複数形にして）

3. The mother read <u>her child</u> many bedtime stories. （下線部を問う疑問文に）

B Rearrange the words in the parentheses to make correct sentences.

4. 日本にある他のどの湖も琵琶湖ほど大きくありません。
   No other (as / large / in Japan / is / lake) as Lake Biwa.

5. 他の医者たちが、がん患者の治療に困っているときに、彼はがんセンターを設立しました。
   He established a cancer centre when other doctors (patients / treating / trouble / with / were having) cancer.

6. 以前はこの駅前にフランス料理レストランがありました。
   There (a French / be / to / restaurant / used) in front of this station.

C Fill in the missing words to complete each sentence.

7. 1つは父へのプレゼントで、もう1つは母へのプレゼントです。
   (   ) is a present for Dad, and (   ) (   ) is a present for Mum.

8. 電車の中で立っている乗客は、自分がスリに盗まれたことに全然気づきませんでした。
   The passenger (   ) on the train never (   ) himself being (   ) (   ) the pickpocket.

5 Look and Write

As you look at the illustration below, fill in the blanks in the paragraph that follows with words from the box. Change the word's form where necessary.

> opinion   paper   photo   question   story   time

A lady reporter who worked at the local ₁(   ) came to interview Ted. She wanted to know how Ted had become an engineer. He said that when he was little, his father spent more ₂(   ) talking to him about rocket engines than reading bedtime ₃(   ). Now, ask yourself a couple of ₄(   ). Why did the woman ask for an old ₅(   ) of Ted's father? What strange thing did she do when Ted was out of the room? Perhaps your ₆(   ) of this young woman reporter is starting to change.

Grammar Check

名詞

1. 数えられる名詞（可算名詞）

普通名詞 (book, desk, hotel)
・不定冠詞 (a /an)、定冠詞 (the) が付くか、または複数形になります。

Is there **a** convenience store nearby?（近くにコンビニがありますか）
Jordan has **a** yacht.（ジョーダンはヨットを持っています）
The books on **the** shelf are new.（棚の本は新刊です）

集合名詞 (people, family, police)

The police are investing the case.（警察はその事件を捜査しています）
☞ police は常に複数扱い

2. 数えられない名詞（不可算名詞）

固有名詞 (Europe, Brown)、物質名詞 (water, equipment)、抽象名詞 (advice, information)
・baggage, luggage, furniture, equipment, news は不可算名詞
・不定冠詞 (a / an) をつけたり複数形にしません。

{ × I have **a** good news for you.
{ ○ I have good news for you.（良い知らせがあります）

{ × Can you give me some informations about the flights?
{ ○ Can you give me some information about the flights?（フライトに関する情報をくれますか）

3. 数えられない名詞の数え方

Let me give you a **piece of** advice.（一言アドバイスさせてください）
I drank **two bottles of** beer at a Japanese-style pub.（居酒屋でビールを 2 本飲みました）
☞ **a cup of** coffee, **a glass of** orange juice, **a sheet of** paper, etc.

Unit 5 The Police Are Puzzled.   comparisons

Warm-up

Listen and fill in the blanks with the words. Then choose the statement (A) or (B) that describes what you see in the picture.

(A) The technicians are (   ) the computer.

(B) The people are (   ) the document together.

   Answer (   )

1 Reading

Read the passage below and then do the exercises that follow.

　　There were some puzzled faces at the meeting at the police station. The police had been working on the Northfield hit-and-run case for nearly a week already, but it was growing more and more mysterious each day. The chief was talking.

　　"What do we know about the victim? Almost nothing! She didn't have a phone or any ID. That alone makes the case stranger than fiction. Why would a young woman be walking around a big—and dangerous—city empty handed? Why was she in Northfield in the first place? Now, I know that at least half a dozen of you did a fingertip search of the scene and surroundings. But you found nothing—nothing at all. No broken glass, no bits of chrome or any other car parts. What does that mean?"

　　"Did an accident really take place or not? If there was no accident, how and why was she so badly injured? And how did she end up 10 metres away in a car park? She's not a bird. She didn't fly there! When she was brought to the hospital—unconscious—we noticed that her shoes were badly scratched and that she had two broken fingernails. Why?"

　　After a pause, the chief then continued. "Now here's what I want you to do. Work in pairs and try once more to see if you can find any witnesses. Re-visit all the local residents and ask them the same questions over again to see if there are any changes in their stories. Re-examine the security cameras. Oh, and David, go back to the office building whose car park we found the woman in and talk to everyone again."

Notes　empty handed「手ぶらで」　　in the first place「まず第一に、そもそも」　　fingertip search 「遺留捜査」　　car part「車の部品」　　in pairs「ペアを組んで」　　security camera「防犯カメラ」

Exercises

A Vocabulary

Match the words on the left below with their meanings (a-e) on the right. Write the letters of each meaning on the lines.

1. surroundings _____	a. a person who is the leader of a group
2. chief _____	b. a person who lives in a town, city, or area
3. scratch _____	c. a person who sees an accident or crime as it takes place
4. witness _____	d. the area around a place
5. resident _____	e. to injure the skin or surface with something sharp

B True or False

Choose the word in bold that correctly completes each sentence. Then, based on the information in the reading passage, circle T if the sentence is true or F if it is false.

1. Every day, the police were becoming more (**puzzling** / **puzzled**) by the case. T F
2. In the road, the police found some tiny (**piece** / **pieces**) of a damaged car. T F
3. The woman had two (**breaking** / **broken**) fingers. T F

C Choosing

Choose the correct answer (A) or (B) for each question below.

1. What information have the police got so far about the victim's identity?
   (A) Her name and age   (B) Almost none

2. What kind of search did the police carry out?
   (A) A very thorough one   (B) A very quick one

3. Why does David have to interview the people in the office building?
   (A) Because the chief thinks the woman works there.
   (B) Because the victim was found in the building's car park.

2 Conversation

A Q&A   20   21

Listen to the conversation with three speakers. Then listen to each question and fill in the blanks, and choose the best answer.

1. _____ _____ the police chief feel about the case?
   (A) He feels angry because there has been almost no progress.
   (B) He is optimistic that the case will be solved soon.
   (C) He is thinking of giving up completely.

2. What is the policeman _____?
   (A) The woman was driving the car herself.
   (B) There is more to this case than they have discovered so far.
   (C) They are very close to solving the mystery.

3. What is the secretary's _____ _____ the new idea?
   (A) She doesn't think the policeman is right.
   (B) She feels very sorry for the victim.
   (C) She thinks she knows the victim.

B L&F

Now, as you listen to the conversation again, fill in the blanks.

chief: I'm annoyed. I've been working harder than ever before on this case, but I am getting nowhere. This is the 1(   ) difficult case I've ever had.

secretary: Do you need more people to 2(   ) you?

chief: Actually, I think I need some luck. Something about this injured woman is not quite right.

policeman: You know what? I don't think she was injured on the 3(   ).

chief: Do you mean she was beaten up somewhere and then 4(   ) in the car park?

policeman: That's a possibility, isn't it?

secretary: It makes me feel 5(   ) just thinking about it. I'm sorry for her.

3 Text Completion

Select the best choice for each numbered blank in the text below.

The mystery woman was the topic of our meeting today. She is still too ill to have visitors, so we are working from an artist's sketch of her. I would say that she is in her late 20s or maybe in her ---1.--- 30s, and not very tall. Her hands are ---2.--- than mine, so she is not a manual worker. Her face has fine features, you know, like ... a nice nose, good skin, and full lips. She is probably quite ---3.--- when she is not lying in a hospital bed. ---4.---

1. (A) early
   (B) fast
   (C) first
   (D) before

2. (A) soft
   (B) softer
   (C) softest
   (D) more soft

3. (A) atrraction
   (B) atrracted
   (C) attracting
   (D) attractive

4. (A) I wish she would wake up and tell us who she is.
   (B) He is sleeping soundly.
   (C) No wonder her hair needs combing.
   (D) My life would be better if I looked just like him.

4 Writing

A Rewrite each sentence below according to the instructions.

1. Some faces at the meeting were puzzled. (There で始めて、puzzled faces を使った文に)

2. The police have been working on the <u>hit-and-run case</u> for a week.
   (下線部を問う疑問文に)

3. No other officer in the police station is smarter than David.
   (David で始めて最上級を使った文に)

B Rearrange the words in the parentheses to make correct sentences.

4. 学生たちはその問題をペアで議論し、それからアイデアをクラスで共有するでしょう。
   Students will discuss (and then / in / pairs / share / the questions) their ideas with the class.

5. 負傷した患者を診察するために、医者が呼ばれました。
   The doctor was (called / examine / in / the injured / to) patient.

6. 私たちの6人が司法試験に合格し、今は弁護士として働いています。
   Half a (of / dozen / passed / the bar examination / us) and now work as lawyers.

C Fill in the missing words to complete each sentence.

7. その事件は地元住民にとって日ごとに、さらに当惑するものになりました。
   The case became more (   ) to the local (   ) each (   ).

8. 彼が病院に運び込まれたとき、彼のためのベッドは全然ありませんでした。
   When he was (   ) into the hospital, (   ) was (   ) bed for him (   ) all.

5 Look and Write

As you look at the illustration below, fill in the blanks in the paragraph that follows with words from the box. Change the word's form where necessary.

> cook   hole   how   pour   rough   sit

This is the BEC foundry. This is the place where workers — like the man 1(   ) outside, taking a break — make steel. His name is Brian and he knows 2(   ) to mix molten steel perfectly. He is like a genius chef 3(   ) up a five-star meal! The hot liquid steel is 4(   ) into moulds and then, when it cools, we can see its 5(   ) shape. Other workers will cut it, shape it, and drill 6(   ) in it to make it into a shiny precision part for a rocket engine.

Grammar Check

比較表現

1. **同等比較：as ＋ 形容詞・副詞の原級 ＋ as**
   Ryan is **as** diligent **as** the other colleagues. （ライアンは他の同僚と同じぐらい勤勉です）
   Stella speaks Spanish **as** fluently **as** English.
   （ステラは、英語と同じようにスペイン語を流暢に話します）

2. **比較級：比較級 ＋ than**
   Dylan cooks better **than** she / her. （ディランは彼女よりも上手く料理をします）
   The phone is more expensive **than** I thought. （その電話は思ったよりも値段が高いです）

3. **最上級：the ＋ 最上級**
   Mason's design was **the** best of all. （メイソンのデザインがみんなの中で一番良かったです）
   Grace is **the** most reliable person in the office. （グレイスはオフィスで一番信頼できる人です）

比較級・最上級の作り方

<規則変化>	原級	比較級	最上級
・原級に -er, -est	high	higher	highest
・語尾が -e は -r, -st	nice	nicer	nicest
・子音＋y は y を i にして -er, -est	busy	busier	busiest
・短母音＋子音は 子音を重ねて -er, -est	hot	hotter	hottest
2 音節以上の語は more, most	careful	more careful	most careful
<不規則変化>	good	better	best
	bad	worse	worst
	little	less	least

Unit 6 Two Witnesses   adjectives / adverbs

Warm-up

Listen and fill in the blanks with the words. Then choose the statement (A) or (B) that describes what you see in the picture.

(A) A lot of people are (   ) the road in front of a new building.

(B) Some taxis are (   ) in line in front of an old building.

Answer (   )

1 Reading

Read the passage below and then do the exercises that follow.

   Bob Castleford is a veteran taxi driver. He is talking to a Northfield police inspector about something that happened on Monday evening. "A woman was standing at the entrance to the new industrial estate," Bob said. "She stopped me, got into my cab, and asked me to take her to the shopping centre on Northfield Road, which I did. I didn't really get a very good look at her, but I know that she was young and not very tall. One thing I did notice, though, was that she had lovely, long, straight hair. She kept playing with it and pulling out loose hairs. And, oh yeah, one more thing. I thought it was pretty strange that she wanted to go to the shopping centre. It was closing time there for all the shops."

   Mrs Lilly Buttercup is an elderly lady who lives alone, in a flat opposite where the accident took place. She, too, is talking to a police officer. "I was watching TV. It was my favourite quiz programme, which starts at 7:30 p.m. on Monday. I heard a noise, but it was only the middle-aged man who lives on the top floor coming home. But then I heard another noise. It came from outside. I looked out my window and saw a big, grey car. It slowed down for a second, but didn't stop. But it was long enough for me to see that the driver was a young man with short, spiky hair…. Oh now, where are my glasses? Ah, here they are. I can't see a thing without them, and I lose them all the time. Last week, I misplaced them on Sunday and didn't find them again until Tuesday morning! That's why I didn't see the accident very clearly on Monday."

Notes police inspector「警部」   industrial estate「工業団地」   get a very good look at「～をとてもしっかり見る」   loose hair「ほつれ髪」   slow down「速度を落とす」   for a second「一瞬」   spiky hair「スパイキーヘア」髪の先をツンツン立てたヘアスタイル。   all the time「いつも」

Exercises

A Vocabulary

Match the words on the left below with their meanings (a-e) on the right. Write the letters of each meaning on the lines.

1. entrance _____
2. notice _____
3. lovely _____
4. programme _____
5. misplace _____

a. a TV show
b. a gate that allows access to a building or park
c. beautiful; attractive
d. to lose something, usually a small object
e. to see or become aware of

B True or False

Choose the word in bold that correctly completes each sentence. Then, based on the information in the reading passage, circle T if the sentence is true or F if it is false.

1. The young woman's hair made a (**good** / **best**) impression on Bob. T F
2. Lilly lives with her husband (**opposite** / **opposition**) the industrial estate. T F
3. The driver of the grey car was a middle- (**age** / **aged**) man with long hair. T F

C Choosing

Choose the correct answer (A) or (B) for each question below.

1. Whose story is more believable, Bob's or Lilly's?
   (A) Bob's   (B) Lilly's

2. What did Bob notice about the young woman?
   (A) She often played with her hair.   (B) She was quite tall.

3. Why wasn't Lilly able to see the accident very well?
   (A) It was after dark.   (B) She wasn't wearing her glasses.

2 Conversation

A Q&A

 24 25

Listen to the conversation. Then listen to each question and fill in the blanks, and choose the best answer.

1. _____ _____ Bob do?
   (A) He is a cab driver.   (B) He is a policeman.
   (C) He works at a shopping centre.

2. How long has Bob been doing _____ _____?
   (A) He started recently.   (B) On Monday evening   (C) Since 1985

3. What was Bob's _____ _____ that woman?
   (A) She looked serious.   (B) She seemed to be worried.
   (C) She was a beautiful person.

B L&F

Now, as you listen to the conversation again, fill in the blanks.

inspector: How long have you been a ₁(   ) driver, Bob?
Bob: Since 1985.
inspector: Do you think you have a ₂(   ) memory for faces?
Bob: Well, yes and no, but that lady was ₃(   ).
inspector: What do you mean?
Bob: She was beautiful. She had long, black, ₄(   ) hair, dark eyes, and a ₅(   ) mouth.
inspector: Um. I see what you mean.

3 Text Completion

Select the best choice for each numbered blank in the text below.

I've been looking in the paper for cars for sale. I want a secondhand car, but one that looks good and runs -------. Ah, here's one. It says the owner is an elderly woman who uses it for shopping only. She is a non-smoker and she drives -------. It is a 1500, with a stereo and an air conditioner, and it's an automatic. She wants £4,500 for it. I think I'll give her a call and ------- her to lower the price. -------

1. (A) good
   (B) correct
   (C) quick
   (D) well

2. (A) care
   (B) careful
   (C) carefully
   (D) careless

3. (A) get
   (B) have
   (C) make
   (D) let

4. (A) I'd better hurry before somebody else buys it.
   (B) He wants to sell the car cheaply.
   (C) Where's my driving license?
   (D) I wonder where he goes shopping.

4 Writing

A Rewrite each sentence below according to the instructions.

1. Kitty stared <u>careful</u> at her baby's <u>sleep</u> face.（下線の語を適切な形にして）

2. Barbara has <u>beautifully</u> blonde <u>curl</u> hair.（下線の語を適切な形にして）

3. The middle-aged man is talking to <u>a police inspector</u>.（下線部を問う疑問文に）

B Rearrange the words in the parentheses to make correct sentences.

4. 被害者は犯人をよく見なかったと言いました。
   The victim (at / didn't / look closely / said / she) the criminal.

5. タクシードライバーは、私の祖父のようにかなり年配の男性でした。
   The taxi driver is (an old / like / man / my grandfather / quite).

6. 会議中に鳴り始めたのは、彼女のスマートフォンでした。
   It (her smartphone / ringing / started / that / was) in the meeting.

C Fill in the missing words to complete each sentence.

7. メガネがどこにあるのか分かりません。
   I don't know (　　　　) my (　　　　) (　　　　).

8. インタビューの間、クレイグは3人の面接官と向かい合って座りました。
   (　　　　　　) the interview, Craig (　　　　) down (　　　　　　) three (　　　　　　).

5 Look and Write

As you look at the illustration below, fill in the blanks in the paragraph that follows with words from the box. Change the word's form where necessary.

> behind   carry   over   noisy   spacious   traditional

There aren't many of these old style cabs on the road these days. Almost all the taxi companies and owner-drivers have changed 1(   ) to new hybrid cars. The new ones are fast, quiet, and economical, but I still love the old London 2(   ) cabs. They were quite slow and 3(   ), but they could turn round in a tiny space, and they were 4(   ) inside. There was plenty of space for luggage, which was 5(   ) at the front, and there was a window 6(   ) the driver, so there was privacy for the passengers.

Grammar Check

形容詞

1. 性質形容詞：性質、状態、種類を表す形容詞
   Online shopping is very convenient for us.（オンラインショッピングは私たちには大変便利です）
   Bennett always wears a nice jacket.（ベネットはいつも素敵なジャケットを着ています）
   I'd like to drink something hot.（何か温かいものを飲みたいです）
2. 数量形容詞：数、量、程度を表す形容詞
   How many times do you go on a business trip each year?（毎年、何回出張しますか）
   Kevin has much experience in automobile designing.（ケビンは自動車の設計に多くの経験があります）
3. 代名形容詞：所有代名詞、指示代名詞、疑問詞を形容詞的に用いたもの
   I will explain about this graphic again.（この図表をもう一度説明します）
   Which computer do you like better?（どちらのコンピュータがお気に入りですか）

副詞

・動詞・形容詞・副詞・文全体を修飾
   William still remembers the story vividly.（ウィリアムはまだそのストーリーをはっきりと憶えています）
   Ava is very strict with us.（アバは私たちにとても厳しいです）
   Natalie is playing soccer fairly well.（ナタリーはかなり上手くサッカーをしています）
   Obviously, Grace is a gifted artist.（明らかに、グレイスは才能のある芸術家です）

Unit 7 The Car Driver   *future / present perfect*

Warm-up

Listen and fill in the blanks with the words. Then choose the statement (A) or (B) that describes what you see in the picture.

(A) The man is (   ) the steering wheel.

(B) The man is (   ) his seatbelt.

   Answer (   )

1 Reading

Read the passage below and then do the exercises that follow.

  Here is what a man named Billy has to say about the incident. "I've only been working there for two weeks or so—doing odd jobs and some driving for my boss. A couple of days ago, she called me into her office and asked me to pick her up just before the Northfield traffic lights on Monday evening at 8:00. 'If I'm not there,' she said, 'drive around the block a couple of times.' It was after my regular working hours, but I told her I'd be there. She's pretty nice, and I need the job."

  "That evening, I was a little early on my first run, but the next time I drove past, there were police and an ambulance right there. I couldn't clearly see what was happening because everyone was crowded round something or someone at the edge of the car park. I wasn't going to hang around—not with all those 'boys in blue' there. So I gave up and came home."

  "In the morning I saw a report on TV and guessed that something had happened to my boss. But what? I'm not really sure. Anyway, she hasn't been in her office since that evening."

  "Would you believe it? I haven't done anything wrong since I was released from prison. And I definitely don't want to get mixed up in anything again. But you know what? Because you're the only person who has really listened to me, I'll give you something to think about. What do my boss and BEC—you know, that engineering company—have in common? Something is going on there."

> **Notes** odd jobs「雑用」   pick ... up「〜を迎えに行く」   first run「1周目」   hang around「ぶらぶらする」
> boys in blue「警察官」   would you believe it?「信じてもらえないかもしれませんが」   release
> from prison「勾留から釈放する」   get mixed up in「〜に関わり合う」   you know what?「あ
> のね」   in common「共通して」

Exercises

A Vocabulary

Match the words on the left below with their meanings (a-e) on the right. Write the letters of each meaning on the lines.

1. incident _____
2. definitely _____
3. block   _____
4. edge   _____
5. release   _____

a. an area of a city with streets on all four sides
b. happening; occurrence
c. surely; for sure
d. the outside part of something; rim
e. to let go

B True or False

Choose the word in bold that correctly completes each sentence. Then, based on the information in the reading passage, circle T if the sentence is true or F if it is false.

1. Billy hasn't been (**worked** / **working**) for his boss for very long.   T F
2. Billy has never been (**in** / **to**) trouble with the police before.   T F
3. BEC actually (**refer** / **refers**) to the engineering company.   T F

C Choosing

Choose the correct answer (A) or (B) for each question below.

1. What did the boss tell Billy to do if she wasn't there?
   (A) To drive around the block   (B) To drive into the car park

2. Why was the pick-up place crowded?
   (A) A concert was taking place.   (B) The police and ambulance staff were there.

3. What is true about Billy?
   (A) He has been working for his boss for several months.
   (B) He has spent some time in prison.

2 Conversation

A Q&A

Listen to the conversation. Then listen to each question and fill in the blanks, and choose the best answer.

1. What does "_____" _____?
   (A) Working without getting paid   (B) Having nothing to do
   (C) Staying in the office

2. Where does the woman want to _____ _____?
   (A) She wants to go to an address in Northfield.
   (B) She wants to go to her office.
   (C) She wants Billy to take her out to dinner.

3. How will they meet when she has _____ _____ business?
   (A) He will drive around and find her.
   (B) He will stand and wait for her next to his car.
   (C) She will phone him on his cellphone.

B L&F

Now, as you listen to the conversation again, fill in the blanks.

woman: Billy, are you free tonight?
Billy: Yes. What would you like me to do?
woman: Can you pick me up here at 6:45 and ₁(   ) me to this address in Northfield?
Billy: Yes, sure. What does the memo say? Ah ... 21 Northfield Avenue. I know ₂(   ) that is.
woman: Oh, and can you pick me up at 8:00 at the same ₃(   )? You don't have to wait for me. Just drive round the block and you should see me.
Billy: Sure. I've ₄(   ) that. So, see you later.
woman: Oh, Billy, I've ₅(   ) my mind. I'll take a taxi there, but make sure you come and pick me up at 8:00.

3 Text Completion

Select the best choice for each numbered blank in the text below.

Last year Pete and I drove through France for a few days. The country was great, but the car broke down. This summer, I really want to get away from England and find some sunshine. I ------- have two weeks off work, but I just don't know where to go. I've ------- to Italy and the south of France, but I ------- been to the Alps yet. I could get a rail pass, go to Switzerland, and ride a train up into the mountains. Hey, that sounds like a good idea! -------
1.   2.   3.   4.

1. (A) am going
   (B) try
   (C) wish
   (D) will

2. (A) be
   (B) been
   (C) went
   (D) gone

3. (A) didn't
   (B) don't
   (C) haven't
   (D) never

4. (A) The Alps are mountains in Switzerland.
   (B) I've been told that the mountain trains are excellent.
   (C) I hate mountain climbing.
   (D) One European rail pass, please.

4 Writing

A Rewrite each sentence below according to the instructions.

1. Nick hung around on the street yesterday. （yesterday を tomorrow にして未来形に）

   _____

2. The CEO is in his office at lunch. （at を since にして現在完了形に）

   _____

3. The salesperson has been working here <u>for five years</u>. （下線部を問う疑問文に）

   _____

B Rearrange the words in the parentheses to make correct sentences.

4. 舞台で何が起こっているのか、はっきりとは見えませんでした。

   I couldn't (happening / on / see clearly / was / what) the stage.

   _____

5. その学生は挨拶をしないで先生のそばを通り過ぎました。

   The student (his teacher / past / saying / walked / without) hello.

   _____

6. フロリダの祖父母に何かがあったのではと心配でした。

   I was (happened / something / that / had / worried) to my grandparents in Florida.

   _____

C Fill in the missing words to complete each sentence.

7. 彼女の大学での専攻と仕事に共通しているのは何ですか。

   (_____) do her college (_____) and her job have in (_____)?

8. 図書館でぶらぶらしている学生もいますし、スマホを見ている学生もいます。

   Some students are (_____) around at the (_____), and others are (_____) at their (_____).

5 Look and Write

As you look at the illustration below, fill in the blanks in the paragraph that follows with words from the box. Change the word's form where necessary.

> difficult   leave   on   opposite   watch   what

Lilly is getting old, and it is more and more ₁(　　　　) for her to go out and to go shopping. This means that Lilly spends a lot of time ₂(　　　　) TV or looking out of her living room window. She lives ₃(　　　　) Ted Bryson's office. She usually knows when a person comes and ₄(　　　　), but she doesn't know ₅(　　　　) the person was doing there. She knew that Mr Bryson had a young woman visitor ₆(　　　　) Monday evening, but she didn't see when the woman left.

Grammar Check

未来形

1. **will**　今決めたこと、不確実な未来の予測
   I will turn on the air conditioner.（エアコンをつけます）
   I will phone him when I get to the office.（オフィスに着いたら彼に電話します）
2. **be going to** すでに決まっている近い未来の予定
   I am going to see the engineer tomorrow.（明日技術者に会います）
   This train is going to leave at 8:00 a.m.（この列車は午前 8 時に出ます）
3. 現在形、現在進行形で未来を表現
   The meeting is at 10.30 a.m. [=will be]（会議は午前 10 時半です）
   I think she is arriving this evening. [= is going to arrive]（彼女は今夜到着すると思います）
   What time does the game start today? [=will the game start]（試合は今日何時に始まりますか）

完了形

1. 現在完了形：現在までの完了・経験・継続 ＜ **have/ has** ＋過去分詞＞
   Lillian has just got to the venue.（リリアンは会場にちょうど着いたところです）
   I have been to Adelaide before.（以前にアデレイドへ行ったことがあります）
   It has been cloudy for a week.（1 週間曇りです）
2. 過去完了形：過去のある時点までの完了・経験・継続 ＜ **had** ＋過去分詞＞
   When Owen arrived at the station, the train had already left.
   （オーウェンが駅に着いたとき、電車はすでに出ていました）
3. 未来完了形：未来のある時点における完了・経験・継続 ＜ **will** ＋ **have** ＋過去分詞＞
   We will have finished the project by Friday.（金曜日までにそのプロジェクトを終えているでしょう）

Unit 8 Office Security *passive voice / causative*

Warm-up

Listen and fill in the blanks with the words. Then choose the statement (A) or (B) that describes what you see in the picture.

(A) The woman is (   ) the door with her key.

(B) The woman is (   ) the panel with her card.

Answer: (   )

1 Reading

Read the passage below and then do the exercises that follow.

　Ted Bryson was taken aback when a detective showed up at the BEC office. Ted had seen the news on TV about the hit-and-run accident, but it had never occurred to him that there might be a connection to his company. But in fact, the young victim had been found in the car park next to Ted's office building.

　Ted described his company's business to the detective, who warned Ted that his documents might be a target for thieves. Ted had to tell the detective everything he had done that Monday, the evening of the accident. Ted explained that he had finished work at about 7:30 and locked his papers up in his steel desk as usual. He had then left the office, locking the door on his way out.

　He was walking to the station, when he remembered that the weather forecast that morning had said that it would rain later in the evening. Ted had left his umbrella back in the office, so, not wanting to get soaked, he turned around and headed back to the company building.

　As he approached the building from the street, he noticed that the lights in his office had not been turned off. He went inside, checked all the lights and windows, and found that the door leading out to the balcony was unlocked. So he locked that, made sure the lights and windows were all OK once again, and, umbrella in hand, left and went to the station to catch his train home.

Notes be taken aback「びっくりする」　show up「現れる」　as usual「いつものように」　on one's way out「出て行くときに」　get soaked「濡れる」

Exercises

A Vocabulary

Match the words on the left below with their meanings (a-e) on the right. Write the letters of each meaning on the lines.

1. detective   _____
2. connection _____
3. describe   _____
4. warn   _____
5. thief   _____

a. a person who steals something
b. a police officer whose job is to find information
c. something that joins two things
d. to say what something or someone is like
e. to tell a person about a possible danger

B True or False

Choose the word in bold that correctly completes each sentence. Then, based on the information in the reading passage, circle T if the sentence is true or F if it is false.

1. The victim was (**find** / **found**) in Ted's office.   T F
2. There (**was** / **were**) nothing out of the ordinary in what Ted did on Monday.   T F
3. It started to (**rain** / **raining**) heavily, so Ted went back to his office to get his umbrella.   T F

C Choosing

Choose the correct answer (A) or (B) for each question below.

1. Why was Ted surprised when the detective came to the company?
   (A) He had no idea that the accident might be connected to his company.
   (B) Ted had never talked to a policeman in his life before.

2. Why did Ted go back to his office?
   (A) He had forgotten something.   (B) He missed his train home.

3. What did he discover in his office?
   (A) Some people were still working.
   (B) The lights were on and the door to the balcony wasn't locked.

2 Conversation

A Q&A

 32   33

Listen to the conversation. Then listen to each question and fill in the blanks, and choose the best answer.

1. How does Ted _____ _____ the detective's questions?
   (A) He feels that it is no trouble at all to answer them.
   (B) He doesn't like the idea of answering them.
   (C) He doesn't know any of the answers.

2. That evening, who _____ _____ the office door?
   (A) One of the workers had.   (B) Ted had.   (C) No one had.

3. When did Ted notice that the office _____ _____ still on?
   (A) On his way to the station   (B) On his way back to the office from the station
   (C) When he was leaving his office

B L&F   CD 32

Now, as you listen to the conversation again, fill in the blanks.

detective: Mr Bryson, thank you for your time and cooperation.
Ted: That's all right. Anything to ₁(   ).
detective: I have got a few questions to ask you. What time did you finish ₂(   ) on Monday evening?
Ted: On Monday? Let me see. Probably at seven ₃(   ).
detective: When you left your office, had all the doors and windows ₄(   ) locked?
Ted: Well, I had locked them and I thought they had been ₅(   ), but when I returned to the office I saw that the office lights had been left on.
detective: Thank you. On your way out again, did you see anything unusual?
Ted: No, I didn't. I just locked the office door and left.

3 Text Completion

Select the best choice for each numbered blank in the text below.

Angela bought a secondhand car a couple of weeks ago, and she is very ------- with
                                                                          1.
it. It is automatic and really easy to drive. An hour ago, she left it in the supermarket car park and went in to do her shopping. She has just returned to her car and has had a shock. It has -------. A young man with a red face is standing next to the car.
                                  2.
He said that he did it and apologised. Angela ------- him write his contact details
                                                 3.
and said she will send him a repair bill. -------
                                           4.

1. (A) please
   (B) pleased
   (C) pleasing
   (D) pleasure

2. (A) damages
   (B) damaged
   (C) been damaged
   (D) been damaging

3. (A) allowed
   (B) forced
   (C) get
   (D) made

4. (A) He asked for money.
   (B) He told her that she was a bad driver.
   (C) He wrote it down and said of course he'd pay.
   (D) He asked what kind of car it was.

4 Writing

A Rewrite each sentence below according to the instructions.

1. The housekeeper left the door unlocked. (the door を主語にした受動態に)

   _____

2. Michael will take an umbrella in case it rains. (an umbrella を主語にした受動態に)

   _____

3. My boss made me help with the report. (下線の語を主語にした受動態に)

   _____

B Rearrange the words in the parentheses to make correct sentences.

4. エミリーは、くるっと向きを変えて笑い始めました。
   Emily (and / began / round / to / turned) laugh.

   _____

5. ジェームズは旅行中にしたことをすべて上司に話さなければなりません。
   James has to tell (about / did / everything / he / the boss) during his trip.

   _____

6. 野生のイノシシが市役所の隣で発見されました。
   A wild boar (been / discovered / had / to / next) the city hall.

   _____

C Fill in the missing words to complete each sentence.

7. 夜の管理人が仕事に来たとき、泥棒はちょうどオフィスを去ったところでした。
   The thief (   ) just (   ) the office (   ) the night janitor came to work.

8. 私が予想していた通り、オフィスの電気は消されていませんでした。
   The office lights (   ) (   ) been (   ) off as I (   ).

5 Look and Write

As you look at the illustration below, fill in the blanks in the paragraph that follows with words from the box. Change the word's form where necessary.

> fly   have   live   minute   on   response

It was a bit of a mystery right from the start. When the police arrived a few ₁(   ) after the accident, they said it was a hit-and-run. But if you think about it, can a person ₂(   ) all the way from the road to the car park? I've been ₃(   ) in Northfield for most of my life. In the past, if we ever ₄(   ) a problem, all sorts of people would try to help. But this accident's been reported ₅(   ) TV several times, but so far there's been no ₆(   ) from the public at all. Don't people want to help any more?

Grammar Check

受動態

1. 受動態：be 動詞＋過去分詞＋ (by)
   The company **is visited by** many people.（その会社には多くの人が訪れます）
   The meeting **is held** every Wednesday.（会議は毎週水曜日に開催されます）
   Cellphones **cannot be used** while driving.（携帯電話は運転中は使用できません）

2. 使役動詞や知覚動詞を含む文の受動態
   Paul **was made** to wait for one hour.（ポールは1時間待たされました）
   Lucy **was seen** getting on a bus.（ルーシーはバスに乗るところを見られました）

3. by 以外の前置詞を用いる受動態
   Ellie **is known to** everyone.（エリーはみんなに知られています）
   The bench **is made of** wood.（そのベンチは木で作られています）
   The mountain **was covered with** snow.（山は雪で覆われていました）

使役動詞

1. 使役動詞 (have, make, let) ＋目的語＋原形不定詞（動詞の原形）
   His compliments always **make** me **feel** good.（彼のお世辞はいつも私の気分を良くしてくれます）
   Please **let** me **know** when you are free.（いつ空いているか、お知らせください）

2. 使役動詞 (get) ＋目的語＋ to 不定詞
   I **got** my colleague **to help** me with my report.（同僚に報告書を手伝ってもらいました）

3. 使役動詞＋目的語＋過去分詞
   Joan **had** her computer **repaired**.（ジョアンはコンピュータを修理してもらいました）

Unit 9 Her Memory Is Coming Back!   *direct speech / reported speech*

Warm-up

Listen and fill in the blanks with the words. Then choose the statement (A) or (B) that describes what you see in the picture.

(A) The doctor is performing (　　　　) in the hospital.

(B) The doctor is (　　　　) something to his patient.

Answer (　　)

1 Reading

Read the passage below and then do the exercises that follow.

　She has regained consciousness. The young woman told me that her headaches have become less painful and not so frequent, and that her memory is slowly coming back. "But I can't speak very clearly yet," she said. "Sorry. I must sound like a drunk. But I can more or less understand what people are saying to me."

5　She then told me that she had spent the day of the incident in her office putting a customer's file in order. One very important piece of information was missing, she said, and that day, she was going to get her hands on it. "Then I would become a top-rank consultant," she said.

　She had taken a taxi to Northfield, she told me, and had walked the last five minutes
10　to the building in the dark. It was just past 7:30. She found that the new office-door key fitted perfectly, and so did the key to the steel desk. She was looking through a pile of papers when she heard a noise outside the office door. "I soon realised that Ted Bryson had come back!" she said.

　She then went on, "There was no place in the office for me to hide, so I opened the
15　door to the balcony, stepped out, and slowly and quietly pushed the door shut. I didn't have to use a key to go out onto the balcony. I thought I was in luck and was going to get away with it. But Ted suddenly checked the door, found it unlocked, and locked it. After he left, I found that the only way I could escape was to climb across a one-metre gap and down the fire escape. But I slipped and fell!"

Notes　sound like「〜のように聞こえる」　　more or less「だいたい」　　put ... in order「〜を整理する」
　　　　　get one's hands on「〜を手に入れる」　　look through「〜に目を通す」　　a pile of「たくさんの」
　　　　　get away with it「うまく逃げ切る」　　fire escape「非常階段」

Exercises

A Vocabulary

Match the words on the left below with their meanings (a-e) on the right. Write the letters of each meaning on the lines.

1. frequent _____
2. consultant _____
3. hide _____
4. escape _____
5. slip _____

a. a person who gives expert advice
b. happening quite often
c. to flee; to run away
d. to lose one's balance and slide out of position
e. to put oneself out of sight

B True or False

Choose the word in bold that correctly completes each sentence. Then, based on the information in the reading passage, circle T if the sentence is true or F if it is false.

1. The young woman no longer makes any mistakes when she (**speaks** / **spoke**).   T F
2. She drove (**on** / **to**) Northfield in her own car.   T F
3. She opened the balcony door (**from** / **with**) the key.   T F

C Choosing

Choose the correct answer (A) or (B) for each question below.

1. What is true about the woman now?
   (A) She can remember some things.
   (B) She can't understand what people are saying.

2. Why most likely did she walk the last few minutes to the office?
   (A) She didn't want to be seen.   (B) The taxi driver said it was too dark.

3. Why couldn't she leave the office through the front door?
   (A) She had dropped the key.   (B) The door to the balcony had been locked.

2 Conversation

A Q&A

 36   37

Listen to the conversation. Then listen to each question and fill in the blanks, and choose the best answer.

1. Why did the woman _____ _____ onto the balcony?
   (A) Because the balcony door was locked.
   (B) Because there was nowhere to hide in the office.
   (C) Because that's where the key was.

47

2. How did she _____ _____ on the balcony?
   (A) She accidentally locked the door.   (B) She forgot the key.
   (C) Ted locked the door.

3. What does the detective want _____ _____?
   (A) What the woman told the nurses
   (B) Whether Ted came back
   (C) Whether the police officer found any clues

B L&F
CD 36

Now, as you listen to the conversation again, fill in the blanks.

detective: She doesn't talk much to the ₁(   ). How about to you?
policeman: Not much, but yesterday she said she ₂(   ) out onto the balcony.
detective: What ₃(   ) her go outside?
policeman: She said Ted had come back and she also said that there was no place to ₄(   ). So she quickly stepped out onto the balcony and closed the door very quietly.
detective: What happened then?
policeman: Ted locked the balcony door and left.
detective: Have you ₅(   ) the balcony for any clues yet?

3 Text Completion

Select the best choice for each numbered blank in the text below.

When my wife came home, she ------- me that her car had been damaged. She
                                1.
said that a young man had done it. She told me that the man was very sorry, and
that he said he ------- pay for the repairs. "Wow, an honest man! I can hardly believe
                2.
it, but ------- me check his ID," I added. I phoned his number and a voice answered,
        3.
"Thank you for calling. I'm sorry to inform you that this number is not in use. Please
dial again." -------
              4.

1. (A) said
   (B) spoke
   (C) talked
   (D) told

2. (A) is going
   (B) can
   (C) shall
   (D) would

3. (A) compel
   (B) get
   (C) let
   (D) permit

4. (A) It was just as I suspected.
   (B) I'll call again, then.
   (C) The voice was very friendly.
   (D) It's all my wife's fault.

4 Writing

A Rewrite each sentence below according to the instructions.

1. The detective said that he had got his hands on the information.（直接話法に言い換えて）

   _____

2. My doctor said to me, "You won't feel as much pain."（間接話法に言い換えて）

   _____

3. The young woman climbed into the car <u>to escape from the disaster</u>.
   （下線部を問う疑問文に）

   _____

B Rearrange the words in the parentheses to make correct sentences.

4. 前日、ソフィアは一流の起業家になると言いました。
   The day before, Sophia said that (a top-rank / become / entrepreneur / she / would).

   _____

5. 退院するとき、その男性はだいたい歩けるようになっていました。
   When he left the hospital, (could / less / more / or / the man) walk.

   _____

6. 月曜日、イザベラは顧客ファイルを整理して過ごしました。
   On Monday, Isabella spent (file / in / putting / the day / a customer's) order.

   _____

C Fill in the missing words to complete each sentence.

7. ウィリアムは出張から戻ったあと、たくさんの書類と向き合いました。
   After William came back (　　　　) his (　　　　　　) trip, he faced a (　　　　) of papers.

8. ドアをノックする音があったとき、その泥棒は金庫を開けているところでした。
   The thief was (　　　　　) the (　　　　) when (　　　　) was a (　　　　) on the door.

5 Look and Write

As you look at the illustration below, fill in the blanks in the paragraph that follows with words from the box. Change the word's form where necessary.

> badly   break   knock   stand   would   write

When I came back to my car, I had quite a shock. There were not many cars in the car park, yet my car had been 1( ) damaged. The front light was 2( ) and the hood was dented. The whole bumper had been 3( ) off, too. There was a tall, young man 4( ) next to the car. He said that he had done it, and that he 5( ) pay for the repairs. But when I got home and phoned the number he had 6( ) down, I realised that he had lied to me.

Grammar Check

話法

1. 直接話法と間接話法の形
- 直接話法は、話者の発言をそのまま伝えます。
- 間接話法は、人が言ったことを自分の言葉に言い換えて伝えます。

She said, "I am going to copy the document."
She said (that) she was going to copy the document. （彼女は書類をコピーすると言いました）

2. 人称代名詞の変化

He said, "I like your design."
He said (that) he liked my design. （彼は私のデザインが好きだと言いました）

3. 時制の一致
- 間接話法で主節の動詞が過去形のときは、時制を一致させます。

He said to me, "You are perfect for the job."
He told me (that) I was perfect for the job. （彼は私がその仕事にピッタリだと言いました）

4. 命令文の話法の書き換え

She said to me, "Turn off the light."
She told me to turn off the light. （彼女は私に消灯するように言いました）

5. 疑問文の話法の書き換え

He said to me, "Are you tired ?"
He asked me if (whether) I was tired. （彼は私が疲れているのかどうか尋ねました）

Unit 10 Is Ted Bryson a Criminal?   *progressives / auxiliary verbs*

Warm-up

Listen and fill in the blanks with the words. Then choose the statement (A) or (B) that describes what you see in the picture.

(A) The woman is (   ) on the balcony.

(B) The woman is (   ) against the wall.

　 Answer (   )

1 Reading

Read the passage below and then do the exercises that follow.

　Ted was being questioned by a man in a dark suit, who said, "You told your version of events to one of our detectives, but I have my doubts about it. So I want you to tell me everything you know, and don't hold anything back!"

　Ted said of course, and then explained that an international conference was being held in Germany soon and that he was going to have to make an important presentation on innovative designs for high-pressure joints in rocket engines. That's why he had been working until late each day. The man in the suit said, "You knew that the woman wanted your designs, right?"

　"Well," said Ted, "I knew that she would be trying to get them. So it was no surprise to see her hiding on the balcony. I could tell that she had been in the office because I recognised the perfume she was wearing. It's the same one that my wife uses." Ted then went on to say that he locked the balcony door, thinking that the woman would be frightened off by having to spend a night outside. "I thought that it would teach her a lesson not to steal secrets," Ted said.

　The man questioning him then said, "Mr Bryson, I want you to think carefully and to answer my question truthfully. Did you push the woman off the balcony before you locked the balcony door?"

　Ted's heart seemed to stop beating. For a short time he couldn't really hear what the man was saying. Then, finally, in a shaky voice, he said, "No, no. I'm not a bad man. I would never do something like that. But the fact is, she aimed to steal my research. She was going to steal my entire life's work!"

Notes hold ... back「〜を隠す」　international conference「国際会議」　high-pressure joint「高圧継手」
　　　teach ... a lesson「〜に教訓を与える」　in a shaky voice「声を震わせて」

Exercises

A Vocabulary
Match the words on the left below with their meanings (a-e) on the right. Write the letters of each meaning on the lines.

1. latest   _____
2. version   _____
3. innovative _____
4. truthfully _____
5. steal   _____

a. a story told from a particular person's point of view
b. in an honest way
c. new; original; inventive
d. newest or most recent
e. to take something illegally; to rob

B True or False
Choose the word in bold that correctly completes each sentence. Then, based on the information in the reading passage, circle T if the sentence is true or F if it is false.

1. The man in the dark suit (**seems** / **seeming**) to be an important policeman.   T F
2. Ted knew that his wife (**is** / **was**) hiding in the office.   T F
3. Ted had no idea the woman (**would** / **was**) try to steal his wife's secrets.   T F

C Choosing
Choose the correct answer (A) or (B) for each question below.

1. What did the man in the dark suit tell Ted that he had to do?
   (A) Ted must tell his story all over again, and tell everything.
   (B) Ted had to write down the truth on a piece of paper.

2. How did Ted know the woman was in the office?
   (A) He checked her background and knew she was a thief.
   (B) He smelled her perfume, and then saw her on the balcony.

3. How did Ted react to the policeman's final question?
   (A) He wasn't worried about it.   (B) He became quite emotional.

2 Conversation

A Q&A

Listen to the conversation. Then listen to each question and fill in the blanks, and choose the best answer.

1. When he was walking back to the office from the station, _____ _____ Ted feel?
   (A) Confident   (B) Frightened   (C) Lonely

2. What was he _____ _____ when he saw the lights on in the office?
   (A) Many things   (B) Nothing   (C) He can't remember.

3. _____ _____ Ted contact the police?
   (A) He was too frightened to do anything.
   (B) He just didn't think about doing it.
   (C) He wanted to catch the criminal by himself.

B L&F

Now, as you listen to the conversation again, fill in the blanks.

detective: When you were walking back to your office from the station, what were you thinking?

Ted: I was scared. Well, when I saw the lights on, I was thinking about many ₁(   ). How many people are in there? Is the office a dangerous ₂(   ) right now?

detective: When you realised there was only one person in there, did you want to ₃(   ) that person?

Ted: I'm not sure.

detective: Why didn't you ₄(   ) the police?

Ted: You ₅(   ) believe this, but it never occurred to me to do that.

3 Text Completion

Select the best choice for each numbered blank in the text below.

It took a week, but I found out a little more about the young man. He is a local lad and is \-\-\-\-\-\-\-\- quite near to us. He said he was sorry for damaging Angela's car. However, he \-\-\-\-\-\-\-\- afford to pay for the damage because he didn't have much money. He works in a shop and does deliveries at night. If he worked for me, he \-\-\-\-\-\-\-\- earn double his present wage. I think I'll check up on him and then make him an offer. \-\-\-\-\-\-\-\-
  1.   2.   3.   4.

1. (A) live
   (B) lived
   (C) living
   (D) being lived

2. (A) could
   (B) couldn't
   (C) unable
   (D) was able

3. (A) could
   (B) has to
   (C) able to
   (D) used to

4. (A) I hope he's OK, because I quite like the lad.
   (B) It's a secret from Angela.
   (C) I'm Angela's excellent boss.
   (D) He looks like my favourite footballer.

4 Writing

A Rewrite each sentence below according to the instructions.

1. I held back my feelings of wanting to marry the woman. （couldn't を加えた文に）

   _____

2. We attended an international conference in Canada. （現在進行形の文に）

   _____

3. Henry knew she was in the house <u>because he recognised her perfume</u>.
   （下線部を問う疑問文に）

   _____

B Rearrange the words in the parentheses to make correct sentences.

4. おしゃれな服を着た女性が、旅行者をギャラリーの入口で出迎えました。
   The woman (a fancy / in / outfit / the tourists / welcomed) at the gallery entrance.

   _____

5. その医者は画期的ながん治療についてのプレゼンテーションをする予定です。
   The doctor (an innovative / make / on / a presentation / will) cancer treatment.

   _____

6. 泥棒はその高級車を盗もうとして逮捕されました。
   A thief was (steal / caught / the luxury / to / trying) car.

   _____

C Fill in the missing words to complete each sentence.

7. その病院の患者はテレビでニュースを見たいと思いましたが、画面を見ることができませんでした。
   The hospital patient (_____) to (_____) the news on TV, but he (_____) see the screen.

8. このコンピュータは私が家で使用しているのと同じものです。
   This computer is the (_____) as the (_____) that I (_____) (_____) at home.

5 Look and Write

As you look at the illustration below, fill in the blanks in the paragraph that follows with words from the box. Change the word's form where necessary.

> do   job   help   report   watch   why

He didn't seem to be a bad lad, so we ₁(　　　　) him for a few days. His day ₂(　　　　) is in a small supermarket. He packs the shelves, ₃(　　　　) out with the ATMs, and fills in as a cashier. There were no bad ₄(　　　　) at all about him. In the evenings, he drives a van and ₅(　　　　) parcel deliveries until quite late. I think he really wanted to pay for Angela's car's repairs. That's ₆(　　　　) I want to give him a chance to work for me.

Grammar Check

> **進行形 be 動詞＋ -ing（現在分詞）**
>
> **1. 現在・過去・完了・未来の進行している動作**
>   Cathy is watching TV now.（キャシーは今テレビを見ているところです）
>   When I called Jenny, she was cleaning her room.
>   （ジェニーに電話をかけたとき、彼女は部屋を掃除していました）
>   Karen has been practicing for the show since this morning.（カレンは今朝からショーの練習をしています）
>   Kevin will be writing his assignment until late at night.（ケビンは夜遅くまで課題を書いているでしょう）
>
> **2. 近い未来**
>   Jackson is leaving for Atlanta tomorrow.（ジャクソンは明日アトランタに向かう予定です）
>   The train is departing in ten minutes.（電車は 10 分後に発車します）
>
> **助動詞**
>
> **1. 主な助動詞 can, could, may, should, must, will, etc.**
>   You should fill out the form carefully.（用紙に注意深く記入するべきです）
>   Guests must leave their bags in the cloakroom.（来客はバッグをクロークに預けなければなりません）
>   Logan will have to call the doctor .（ローガンは医者に電話しなければならないでしょう）
>   Amy will be able to leave hospital soon.（アミーはもうすぐ退院できるでしょう）
>
> **2. ought to, used to**
>   William ought to apologise to her in person.（ウィリアムは彼女に直接謝るべきです）
>   There used to be a fancy restaurant here.（以前ここに高級レストランがありました）

Unit 11 Who Is She?

infinitives / gerunds

Warm-up

Listen and fill in the blanks with the words. Then choose the statement (A) or (B) that describes what you see in the picture.

(A) Passengers are (　　　　　) the train.

(B) Two people on the (　　　　　) carry their backpacks.

　　Answer (　　　)

1 Reading

Read the passage below and then do the exercises that follow.

　　It wasn't too difficult for the police to find the engineering consultancy company that the young woman worked for. It was Billy Blue's advice that led them to her. The police had given Billy that nickname because blue was his favourite colour and he was always wearing something blue.

5 　　The young woman had been born in Croatia, but came to live in England when she was still a teenager. Her father was an engineer, and a very talented one at that. He had what it takes to climb the academic ladder to a position near the top of the field. But in those days, most people around him did not agree to a foreigner becoming so well known, and so important. The woman's father worked hard—too hard—and lived
10 under a lot of stress, and together they killed him.

　　His daughter, Sonia, was heartbroken and bitter, and promised to avenge her father's untimely death. She vowed that she would reach the top of the field instead of her father. What she did not explain to anyone was how she planned to do this.

　　But she herself knew what she had to do. She would use any method, no matter how
15 dishonest or risky, so long as it was quick and it worked—so long as it got her to the top. She wanted Ted Bryson's design—really wanted it! It was the key to everything!

　　Now, Ted is not just your average engineer. As you may have already figured out, Ted is a pretty sharp guy. With a single phone call, he was able to find out that there was no such paper as *The Northfield Gazette*. It had closed down more than two years ago. So the woman reporter was a fake, an impostor.

Notes engineering consultancy company「エンジニアリング・コンサルタント会社」　at that「それも」
　　　　what it takes to「～するのに必要なもの」　academic ladder「アカデミックなはしご」　in those days「その当時は」　bitter「憤慨した」　so long as「～する限り」　figure out「分かる」

Exercises

A Vocabulary

Match the words on the left below with their meanings (a-e) on the right. Write the letters of each meaning on the lines.

1. talented _____
2. avenge _____
3. vow _____
4. risky _____
5. impostor _____

a. a person pretending to be someone else
b. dangerous; not safe
c. having a special ability to do something well
d. to promise; to swear
e. to pay back for something done to hurt you

B True or False

Choose the word in bold that correctly completes each sentence. Then, based on the information in the reading passage, circle T if the sentence is true or F if it is false.

1. Nobody (**know** / **knew**) what Billy's nickname was. T F
2. The woman's father is still living and (**work** / **working**) in England. T F
3. The woman vowed (**to do** / **doing**) anything to become a top engineer. T F

C Choosing

Choose the correct answer (A) or (B) for each question below.

1. Where did the woman come from?
   (A) She was born in England.   (B) She was born in Croatia.

2. What was the attitude towards foreigners in those days?
   (A) They were treated as equals.   (B) They were treated unfairly.

3. How did Ted find out about the woman?
   (A) By learning the newspaper no longer existed   (B) By talking with Billy

2 Conversation

A Q&A

Listen to the conversation with three speakers. Then listen to each question and fill in the blanks, and choose the best answer.

1. How did Billy get _____ _____ a lot about the woman?
   (A) He looks after her mail.   (B) He's known her since she was a kid.
   (C) They spend time together in a car.

2. How does she _____ _____ the engineering association?
   (A) She likes and respects the members.
   (B) She hates them for "killing" her father.
   (C) She wants them to like her.

3. How does she plan to get her own back on _____ _____?
   (A) By appearing on television
   (B) By becoming more famous than them
   (C) By writing a book about the association

B L&F

Now, as you listen to the conversation again, fill in the blanks.

detective: Now then Billy, I think driving the woman around all the time has given you a chance to get to ₁(   ) that lady pretty well.
Billy: Well, I know that she came from Croatia when she was a young ₂(   ).
detective: Well, what else did she tell you?
secretary: Come on, Billy. Tell us what she is doing in England.
Billy: She said that her father had ₃(   ) young, and that she wanted to get her own back on the engineering association.
secretary: Like getting hold of the latest ₄(   )?
Billy: Something like that. It would ₅(   ) her more famous, that's for sure.

3 Text Completion

Select the best choice for each numbered blank in the text below.

After thinking carefully about it for a long time, the young woman decided to steal as many secret documents as possible before she left the country. That was the quickest way ------ about Britain's engineering progress. So she planned
                    1.
------ information from some small but innovative companies. But her big dream
  2.
was ------ access to the testing data for the new high-pressure joints designed by
      3.
an established company like BEC. That information would become the key to her success. ------
              4.

1. (A) creating
   (B) losing
   (C) to leak
   (D) to learn

2. (A) get
   (B) getting
   (C) to get
   (D) to be got

3. (A) giving
   (B) holding
   (C) to enter
   (D) to get

4. (A) It would truly avenge her father's death.
   (B) And then she could marry Billy Blue.
   (C) He knew she would go to prison.
   (D) She thinks she cannot get the information.

4 Writing

A Rewrite each sentence below according to the instructions.

1. It seemed that she had too much stress. （She seemed で始めて、不定詞を用いて）

2. It is said that he is improving his English skills. （He is で始めて、不定詞を用いて）

3. It was difficult for me to make a new design. （下線部を動名詞に代え、主語にして）

B Rearrange the words in the parentheses to make correct sentences.

4. その販売員は、あとで彼女に電話をかけ直すと約束しました。
   The salesperson (call / back / her / promised / to) later.

5. その老婦人は、証拠として何か重要なものを警察に渡しました。
   The old woman gave (as / evidence / important / something / the police).

6. 理事会は、外国人技術者が社長になることに賛成しませんでした。
   The board of directors did not (a foreign / agree / becoming / engineer / to) president.

C Fill in the missing words to complete each sentence.

7. 一生懸命勉強したことで、彼女は第一希望の企業に入ることができました。
   (   ) hard enabled her (   ) get into the company of her (   ) choice.

8. 私の夫は、勤めている会社の頂点への出世階段を駆け上がる可能性があります。
   My husband is likely to (   ) the corporate (   ) to the (   ) of the company he (   ) for.

5 Look and Write

As you look at the illustration below, fill in the blanks in the paragraph that follows with words from the box. Change the word's form where necessary.

decorate   except   leave   thing   view   with

The young woman is recovering nicely, and soon she will be able to 1(   ) the hospital. She has a private room 2(   ) a policeman sitting outside the door day and night. Her room is a little small and simply 3(   ). She has a window, but the 4(   ) is of red-brick buildings and empty windows. The cleaning staff are friendly. They change the bedding and bring 5(   ) to eat and drink. But sadly, the young patient has had no visitors at all, 6(   ) for that young man with the short, spiky hair.

Grammar Check

不定詞と動名詞

1. 不定詞：名詞的用法、形容詞的用法、副詞的用法

To master a new skill is one of the keys to success.
（新しい技能をマスターすることは成功への鍵の1つです）
Lucas has a lot of work to do this week.（ルーカスは今週するべきたくさんの仕事があります）
Tony went to New York to study business.（トニーはビジネスを学ぶためにニューヨークへ行きました）

2. 動名詞：動詞の原形＋ -ing で、文の主語・補語・目的語、前置詞の目的語

Living in this city is exciting.（この都市で住むことは刺激的です）
Next year I'll be studying abroad.（来年留学する予定です）
Young people love trying new things.（若い人は新しいことを試すのが好きです）
I'm looking forward to seeing you again.（また会えることを楽しみにしています）
☞ look forward to の to は前置詞

3. 不定詞のみを目的語にとる動詞、動名詞のみを目的語にとる動詞

不定詞：afford, agree, claim, decide, plan, refuse, want, wish
動名詞：avoid, enjoy, deny, finish, give up, mind, miss, resist
Karen **wants** to buy some new jeans.（カレンは新しいジーンズを買いたいと思っています）
Charles **finished** making the engine parts.（チャールズはエンジン部品の製作を終えました）

4. 不定詞と動名詞で意味が異なる動詞：forget, remember, regret, stop など

Beth **remembers** to do the work.（ベスはその仕事をするのを覚えています）
Peter **remembers** doing the work.（ピーターはその仕事をしたことを覚えています）

Unit 12 Do You Realise Who You Are? *prepositions / conjunctions*

Warm-up

Listen and fill in the blanks with the words. Then choose the statement (A) or (B) that describes what you see in the picture.

(A) The woman is (   ) an email over her computer.

(B) The woman is looking at her computer and (   ) notes.

Answer (   )

1 Reading

Read the passage and then do the exercises that follow.

　Good morning, Ted. Thanks for coming in to my office. I've asked you here today because I have something of vital importance to tell you. It's something that I don't think you have really begun to comprehend. But I am sure that you, better than anyone else, realise that your research and products are at the very top level of the field of engineering in this country.

　Many people domestically and abroad would love to get their hands on your secret papers, or even on you. What I'm saying is that you are an important national asset, not just a local one. You are, in fact, a national security matter, which means that you can no longer look after yourself on your own.

　You need a team of helpers to protect you. My job is to run that team of helpers and to make sure that you and your research are safe and secure. If you ever want to talk to me about anything, just ask for Mark, that's me. I just want you to know that from now on, there will always be someone nearby, keeping a close eye on you. So don't worry about a thing.

　I'll bet you didn't know that you have another pair of eyes. We have an elderly woman in the block of flats opposite your office who keeps a constant eye on you. She logs you in and out, and keeps track of all your visitors. Lilly is old, but she is sharp and dedicated to helping her country. If you ever need help in a hurry, hang a T-shirt in the window of your office, and leave it to Lilly.

> **Notes**　**national security**「国家安全保障」　**look after**「世話をする」　**on one's own**「1人で」　**from now on**「今後は」　**keep a close eye on**「〜を見守る」　**keep a constant eye on**「〜から目を離さない」　**keep track of**「〜の記録を取る」

Exercises

A Vocabulary

Match the words on the left below with their meanings (a-e) on the right. Write the letters of each meaning on the lines.

1. vital _____
2. comprehend _____
3. asset _____
4. secure _____
5. log _____

a. a useful or valuable thing or person
b. protected from danger or harm
c. very important; essential
d. to keep a record of something
e. to understand fully

B True or False

Choose the word in bold that correctly completes each sentence. Then, based on the information in the reading passage, circle T if the sentence is true or F if it is false.

1. The policeman came to Ted's office to speak to him (**in** / **for**) private. T F
2. Mark is the head (**among** / **of**) a team that looks after Ted. T F
3. (**By** / **In**) an emergency, Ted should run over and give Lilly a T-shirt. T F

C Choosing

Choose the correct answer (A) or (B) for each question below.

1. What is the first paragraph mainly about?
   (A) Mark just wants to meet Ted.   (B) Mark has something important to tell Ted.

2. What position does Mark hold in the police department?
   (A) He is not particularly high up.   (B) He is the boss who runs Ted's helpers.

3. What are Lilly's qualifications for her job of being Ted's "other pair of eyes"?
   (A) She is an old and experienced police officer.
   (B) She lives opposite Ted's office and is dedicated to helping her country.

2 Conversation

A Q&A

Listen to the conversation. Then listen to each question and fill in the blanks, and choose the best answer.

1. Why was it _____ _____ Ted to meet the detective this week?
   (A) He is going away on holiday.   (B) He has to be in court all week.
   (C) He will be at a conference in Germany.

2. Why is today the only day the detective _____ _____ with Ted?
   (A) She is working on another case. (B) She has to be in court starting tomorrow.
   (C) Tomorrow is her day off.

3. Why is Ted becoming _____ _____?
   (A) He doesn't trust Mark.   (B) He doesn't know Mark's schedule.
   (C) The situation is becoming complicated.

B L&F

Now, as you listen to the conversation again, fill in the blanks.

detective: Well, hello, Ted. I wanted to spend some time with you, but this week it was a little difficult to squeeze you ₁(   ) my schedule.

Ted: Yeah, me too. From Thursday for four days I'll be at the conference in Germany.

detective: Well, tomorrow and the day after, I have to be ₂(   ) court. So, that only leaves today ₃(   ).

Ted: I was pleased when you said we could have a working lunch.

detective: There is somebody else I want you to meet. Mark is ₄(   ) for you in his office.

Ted: Another person? I'm becoming very confused ₅(   ) all of this.

3 Text Completion

Select the best choice for each numbered blank in the text below.

I got into my car and drove to the new supermarket in Bridgewater Road. I wanted to buy a cake and some flowers because it was my mother's birthday. She was born ------- 1948, so she is getting pretty old. When I was parking my car, I saw
1.
somebody I knew. It was Angela, who works in our office. She was talking ------- a
2.
policeman. She was saying, "The incident was on Monday, ------- about 3:00 in the
3.
afternoon, in this parking space right here." -------
4.

1. (A) at
   (B) for
   (C) from
   (D) in

2. (A) about
   (B) by
   (C) of
   (D) to

3. (A) at
   (B) between
   (C) on
   (D) over

4. (A) Angela's an excellent worker.
   (B) Angela was wearing a really nice dress.
   (C) The policeman was writing something on a notepad.
   (D) I couldn't hear what Angela was saying.

4 Writing

A Rewrite each sentence below according to the instructions.

1. There is somebody who will take care of you.（疑問文に）

   _____

2. Alice was a teenager, and then she moved to California（接続詞 when を使って 1 文に）

   _____

3. It was easy to spot the woman <u>because</u> she wore a red coat.（下線部を前置詞に換えて）

   _____

B Rearrange the words in the parentheses to make correct sentences.

4. 人々が国民の休日を祝うとき、しばしば国旗が玄関に掲げられます。
   When people celebrate national holidays, the national flag (hung / is / often / over / the front) door.

   _____

5. 複雑な秘密のパスワードが、あなたの情報を安全かつ確実に保護しています。
   A complicated secret (and / keeps / password / safe / your information) secure.

   _____

6. 警察官が建物の向かい側のアパートに住んでいて、住民の世話をしています。
   A police officer lives in the flat (after / and / looks / opposite / our building) the residents.

   _____

C Fill in the missing words to complete each sentence.

7. 私の夢は、ニューヨークで和食料理店を経営することです。
   My (　　　　) is to (　　　　) a (　　　　　　) restaurant in New York.

8. アフリカの多くの人々が、その病気の新薬を手に入れて幸せになるでしょう。
   Many people in Africa (　　　　　) be happy to get their (　　　　　) on the new (　　　　　) for the (　　　　　).

5 Look and Write

As you look at the illustration below, fill in the blanks in the paragraph that follows with words from the box. Change the word's form where necessary.

> and   during   in   or   since   wear

I have known Angela ₁(　　　) we were at school. She is an exciting person. If you catch her ₂(　　　) a weekend, you might think she is a man. She ₃(　　　) Wellington boots all day, and jeans with braces. But during the week she is an efficient business lady. She lives in the country ₄(　　　) a small red-brick terraced house. She visits her mother each week and never forgets people's birthdays, anniversaries, ₅(　　　) other special days. Spend some time with Angela ₆(　　　) you will always enjoy yourself.

Grammar Check

前置詞

・時・場所・理由・方法などを表すため、名詞・代名詞の前に置く

Samuel will wait for another half an hour. (サミュエルはさらに30分待つでしょう)
We arrived at the airport in the middle of the night. (私たちは真夜中に空港に着きました)
Emma goes to the supermarket either by bike or on foot. (エマは自転車か徒歩でスーパーへ行きます)
There's something mysterious about her. (彼女には謎めいたところがあります)

接続詞

・語・句・文をつなぐ

1. 等位接続詞：語や句や文を対等に結ぶ (and, but, for, nor, or)

    Kitty likes shopping and travelling. (キティはショッピングと旅行が好きです)
    Tracy wanted to go to a rock concert, but the tickets were sold out.
    (トレイシーはロックコンサートに行きたかったが、チケットが売り切れていました)

2. 従位接続詞：名詞節を導く (if, that, whether)、副詞節を導く (although, as, because, if, since, until, when, while)

    I don't know if Jennifer will come on time. <名詞節>
    (ジェニファーが時間通りに来るかどうか分かりません)
    If it rains tomorrow, we will postpone the event. <副詞節>
    (もし明日雨が降れば、私たちはイベントを延期するでしょう)

Unit 13 How Are You? imperatives / exclamations

Warm-up

Listen and fill in the blanks with the words. Then choose the statement (A) or (B) that describes what you see in the picture.

(A) The woman with the broken leg is sitting in her (   ).

(B) The woman whose leg is in a cast is (   ) with the doctor.

Answer (   )

1 Reading

Read the passage and then do the exercises that follow.

　　The doctor who had been treating Sonia went into her hospital room, sat down next to her bed, and said, "Good morning, Sonia. You are looking very well. I have just gone through the results of the tests we ran on you yesterday, and everything is looking great. So the good news is that you can leave the hospital tomorrow. Of
5 course, until you completely recover, we will need to see you once a week back here to make sure everything is healing properly. How does that sound, Sonia?"

　　"I couldn't be happier. Thanks so much for everything, doctor."

　　"My pleasure. All the medical staff here think you are amazing. Not many people could fall from such a high place, get a serious bump on the head, and then recover as
10 quickly as you have. I checked yesterday's X-rays, and, with just a bit more therapy, you should have full use of that broken arm within two weeks. Your broken leg is also mending quite well, but you still shouldn't put any weight on it for at least three more weeks. The physiotherapist will be showing you how to strengthen it."

　　"Now then, as you know, it was your head injury that was causing some worries.
15 But your headaches are less frequent and less severe now, and you are sleeping better, too. So that's encouraging news. Your face still looks a bit like a boxer's—sorry for the bad joke—but the bruises are fading nicely and should completely disappear very soon. And you'll be back to your lovely self."

　　"Before you are discharged tomorrow, a nurse will come in and explain how to
20 pay your bill and how to claim any insurance you might have. So, see you tomorrow morning, then, Sonia."

> **Notes** go through「調べる」　run「実施する」　leave the hospital「退院する」　medical staff「医療スタッフ」　put any weight on「体重をかける」　physiotherapist「理学療法士」

Exercises

A Vocabulary

Match the words on the left below with their meanings (a-e) on the right. Write the letters of each meaning on the lines.

1. mend _____
2. encouraging _____
3. fade _____
4. discharge _____
5. bill _____

a. a written statement of money owed for a service
b. making a person feel hopeful or positive
c. to allow someone to leave a hospital
d. to disappear gradually
e. to heal or cure

B True or False

Choose the word in bold that correctly completes each sentence. Then, based on the information in the reading passage, circle T if the sentence is true or F if it is false.

1. Sonia will spend two more (**night** / **nights**) in hospital.　　T F
2. The doctor seems to be (**optimist** / **optimistic**) about Sonia's recovery.　　T F
3. Sonia will be asked to settle her bill before she (**leaves** / **left**) hospital.　　T F

C Choosing

Choose the correct answer (A) or (B) for each question below.

1. What is the doctor's main message for Sonia?
   (A) "You may leave the hospital tomorrow."
   (B) "You need a few more tests before you can go."

2. What surprised the hospital staff?
   (A) That Sonia can already walk with no trouble
   (B) That Sonia is getting better so quickly

3. What final things must Sonia do before her discharge?
   (A) She must pay her bill and discuss insurance claims.
   (B) She has to go around and thank all the staff.

2 Conversation

A Q&A

Listen to the conversation. Then listen to each question and fill in the blanks, and choose the best answer.

1. What are the _____ _____?
   (A) She has a fever and headache.
   (B) She is dizzy, feels tired and doesn't eat much.
   (D) She can't really explain how she feels.

2. When will the real _____ _____?
   (A) Immediately   (B) When the patient is willing to start
   (C) After the doctor has checked the test results

3. When should she make her _____ _____?
   (A) For later this afternoon
   (B) If the results are good, she doesn't need an appointment.
   (C) For Wednesday

B L&F

Now, as you listen to the conversation again, fill in the blanks.

patient: Good morning, doctor.
doctor: Good morning. Now, what's your 1(   ) today?
patient: Well, I feel dizzy, and I get tired 2(   ).
doctor: How long have you been feeling ill?
patient: For three days, and I have no 3(   ) at all.
doctor: OK. I'll run some tests, but I 4(   ) get the results for two days. So I'd like you to come again on Wednesday. In the meantime, I'll give you some medicine that should make you feel better. Take it three 5(   ) a day, and try to eat some soft food.
patient: Yes, doctor. Thank you. See you on Wednesday.

3 Text Completion

Select the best choice for each numbered blank in the text below.

Hey you! What do you think you're ---1.---? Don't touch my car. Stand still and put your hands in the air. Don't ---2.--- I'll hit you. Now, where's my phone? ... Hello? Hello? Is that the police? I've just caught a car thief. ---3.---, he is unarmed, but he has broken the rear door window of my car. I'm in the Walmart car park, near the exit. He is about 16, and quite tall, about 185. He hasn't told me his name yet. ---4.---

1. (A) do
   (B) doing
   (C) did
   (D) done

2. (A) damage, and
   (B) drive off
   (C) move, or
   (D) run away

3. (A) Surprise
   (B) Surprised
   (C) Surprising
   (D) Surprisingly

4. (A) I'm going shopping now.
   (B) He doesn't have a bike.
   (C) She looks hungry and wants some food.
   (D) I don't think it's the first time he's done this.

4 Writing

A Rewrite each sentence below according to the instructions.

1. You must explain what I need to do to leave the hospital. （Please で始まる命令文に）

2. You should not put any weight on your leg for two weeks. （命令文に）

3. What a serous injury this is! （How で始める感嘆文に）

B Rearrange the words in the parentheses to make correct sentences.

4. 私たちが最新の製品に対して実施したテストの結果について、調べてください。
   Please go through (on / ran / results / the test / we) our latest product.

5. その医者は患者が完治するまで、月 2 回診察に来なさいと言いました。
   The doctor told the patient (come and / him / to / twice / see) a month until he completely recovers.

6. そんなに早く腕を使えるようになるなんて、何という驚きだったことでしょう。
   What a (able to / it / surprise / to be / was) use my arm so quickly!

C Fill in the missing words to complete each sentence.

7. 退院する前に、請求書を支払う必要があります。
   Before you are (   ), you will need to (   ) your (   ).

8. あんなに高い所から落ちたら、たいていの人はあなたと同じぐらい早く回復することはないでしょう。
   Most people who (   ) from such a high place would not (   ) as quickly (   ) you (   ) done.

5 Look and Write

As you look at the illustration below, fill in the blanks in the paragraph that follows with words from the box. Change the word's form where necessary.

> control   do   driver   trouble   who   which

Burt is not a hero, not even a special person. He is the kind of man 1( ) does his job conscientiously. Burt looks after the car park and handles all the 2( ) that happen in it. He has been 3( ) this job since the hospital was built, 4( ) is about 30 years ago. When tempers rise and the 5( ) are preparing to fight, Burt comes along, and in a quiet but firm voice takes 6( ) of a tense situation. He is a great guy.

Grammar Check

命令文

- 人に何かを命令、禁止、提案する表現
  1. 肯定の命令文：動詞の原形＋〜「〜しなさい」
     Wait a minute.（ちょっと待ってください）
     Be kind to others.（他人に親切にしてください）
  2. 否定の命令文
     Don't speak so loudly.（そんなに大きな声で話してはいけません）
     Never do such a thing.（決してそのようなことをしてはいけません）
  3. 丁寧な命令文
     Please be careful of your health.（どうぞお体に気を付けてください）
     Be careful not to catch a cold, please.（どうぞ風邪を引かないように注意してください）
  4. 提案の命令文：Let's ＋動詞の原形「〜しよう」
     Let's meet at the café at two.（2時にカフェで会いましょう）

感嘆文

- 驚き、悲しみ、喜びなどの感情を強調して伝える表現
  1. 感嘆文の形
     What + (a / an) +形容詞+名詞+主語+動詞！
     How +形容詞（副詞）＋主語+動詞！
       ☞名詞があるときは What、名詞がないときは How
  2. What と How の書き換え
     What a very good worker he is!
     How well he works!（彼はなんて仕事ができるのでしょう）

Unit 14　A Face in the Crowd　　relatives

Warm-up

Listen and fill in the blanks with the words. Then choose the statement (A) or (B) that describes what you see in the picture.

(A) Customers are (　　　　　) at the checkout counter.

(B) Customers can look into the store through the (　　　　　).

Answer (　　)

1 Reading

Read the passage below and then do the exercises that follow.

　Two burly policemen in dark suits came to the hospital in a police car, ran to the reception desk, and asked the nurse if Sonia was still in the same room. "Yes, sirs," she said, and the two men rushed upstairs. Sonia's room was a private one. A young policeman, one of those who were supposed to be keeping a 24-hour watch on Sonia, was sitting outside. He was reading the horse-racing results in a tightly folded newspaper.

　The two men in suits pushed open the door and looked all round the room. Nothing seemed out of the ordinary. There was her unmade bed. There was the one window, closed. There were some magazines on a bedside table. But the room was empty. The patient was not there. The young guard said that Sonia had just popped around the corner to the supermarket to pick up some ladies' stuff. "She does that every day," he told the two policemen. "She'll be right back. She always is."

　The two policemen nodded and then stood around waiting patiently, not saying a word. The young guard had a worried look on his face. When they had been waiting for over half an hour, a bell went off in the older policeman's head. "We've been bamboozled!" he said.

　They hurried along the corridor to the nurses' station and asked a nurse if she had seen Sonia. "She went out a little while ago," the nurse said, "in her wheelchair, with her driver Billy pushing her." The two policemen then sprinted to the supermarket on the corner and breathlessly asked a salesperson if she had seen Sonia. "Well, not today," she said. "She's usually here every day at this time. But she hasn't shown up today. Not yet anyway."

Notes　**private one**「個室」　　**horse-racing**「競馬」　　**unmade bed**「整えられていないベッド」　　**pick up**「買う」　　**ladies' stuff**「女性に必要なもの」化粧品や生理用品など。　　**nurses' station**「ナースステーション」看護師の詰め所。　　**Not yet anyway.**「とにかくまだです」

Exercises

A Vocabulary

Match the words on the left below with their meanings (a-e) on the right. Write the letters of each meaning on the lines.

1. reception _____
2. burly _____
3. sprint _____
4. patiently _____
5. breathlessly _____

a. a desk in a hospital where visitors first go
b. excitedly; gasping for air
c. strongly built; muscular
d. without becoming annoyed or irritated at a delay
e. to run fast; to dash

B True or False

Choose the word in bold that correctly completes each sentence. Then, based on the information in the reading passage, circle T if the sentence is true or F if it is false.

1. The young police guard was doing his job very (**conscientious** / **conscientiously**). T F
2. Sonia's room was (**for** / **in**) order except for one very important thing. T F
3. The two policemen got to the supermarket just in time (**to catch** / **catching**) Sonia. T F

C Choosing

Choose the correct answer (A) or (B) for each question below.

1. Where was the young police guard sitting?
   (A) Next to the hospital bed
   (B) By the door outside the room

2. What does "a bell went off in the older policeman's head" in line 14 mean?
   (A) The policeman suddenly realised something.
   (B) The policeman was getting tired of waiting.

3. What did the salesperson at the supermarket think was unusual today?
   (A) Sonia hadn't appeared at the supermarket.
   (B) Sonia was being pushed by another person, not Billy.

2 Conversation

A Q&A

Listen to the conversation. Then listen to each question and fill in the blanks, and choose the best answer.

1. Even though Sonia couldn't walk, _____ _____ did she make?
   (A) She seemed to be in control of the situation.
   (B) She was very open and friendly.
   (C) She loved talking to anyone she met.

2. Why would it be difficult for Sonia _____ _____ from the hospital?
   (A) Her face has often been shown on TV.
   (B) She would need help because she can't move on her own well.
   (C) Her wheelchair wasn't working properly.

3. How does the policeman _____ _____ Sonia?
   (A) She is quite good-looking.
   (B) She is a professional.
   (C) She is lucky to be alive.

B L&F

Now, as you listen to the conversation again, fill in the blanks.

policeman: What impression did you have when Sonia was shopping?
salesperson: Even though she was in a wheelchair and couldn't move by herself very well, she always ₁(   ) cool and confident. I think it was difficult for her to come here from the hospital.
policeman: What kind of clothes did she ₂(   )?
salesperson: Only her usual hospital ₃(   ), you know, pajamas, a dressing gown, and slippers.
policeman: Did she talk to you?
salesperson: Well, come to think of it, no, not one ₄(   ).
policeman: It's no wonder we couldn't ₅(   ) her. Sonia is a real professional.

3 Text Completion

Select the best choice for each numbered blank in the text below.

Burt has been working in the hospital for 30 years. He is the man ------- looks after the car park. He is just a normal-looking guy, but he is really good at his job. For example, yesterday, he was the only guy who ------- stop two drivers who were arguing about a parking space. Some drivers are nasty people. That's ------- the car park has security cameras all over the place. If a driver sneaks away after an accident, Burt will probably catch up with him or her. -------

1. (A) who
   (B) whose
   (C) whom
   (D) which

2. (A) managed to
   (B) manages to
   (C) managing to
   (D) manage

3. (A) how
   (B) where
   (C) why
   (D) when

4. (A) I never park there myself.
   (B) One of the cameras is broken.
   (C) Now Burt's taking care of his two children.
   (D) The car park is really lucky to have a worker like Burt.

4 Writing

A Rewrite each sentence below according to the instructions.

1. Look at the flowers. My parents brought them. （関係代名詞 that を使って1文に）

   _____

2. There was a policeman. He guarded the patient in the hospital.
   （関係代名詞 who を使って1文に）

   _____

3. The policemen searched the park. The suspect was there. （関係副詞 where を使って1文に）

   _____

B Rearrange the words in the parentheses to make correct sentences.

4. トムは車いすの女性が道路を渡るのを手伝いました。
   Tom helped (her wheelchair / in / the woman / was / who) cross the road.

   _____

5. 刑事は私にその中年男性が以前ここにいたことがあるかどうか尋ねました。
   The detective asked me (been / had / here / if / the middle-aged man) before.

   _____

6. その医者は一番上の棚にある数冊の本を降ろしました。
   The doctor (on / pulled down / were / some books / that) the top shelf.

   _____

C Fill in the missing words to complete each sentence.

7. 看護師は医者の診察を受けている母親の赤ん坊の世話をします。
   The nurse will (　　　　　) after the baby (　　　　　) mother is (　　　　　) the doctor.

8. 警察が銀行に到着するまでに、強盗はスピードの出るSUV車ですでに逃走していました。
   By the time the police (　　　　　) at the bank, the robbers (　　　　　) already (　　　　　) their escape in a (　　　　　) SUV.

5 Look and Write

As you look at the illustration below, fill in the blanks in the paragraph that follows with words from the box. Change the word's form where necessary.

> around   down   even   help   look   thing

Take a good look at the guy in the picture. He is Billy. When he comes into the story, he is always ₁(   ) someone. His job is to help Sonia in the office and to drive her ₂(   ), but he also helps the police. He seems to like them, ₃(   ) though they put him in prison for a short time. He has a great nickname and ₄(   ) smart with his sunglasses and spiky hair. Sonia seems to be a bit ₅(   ). Maybe ₆(   ) are not going to plan, or maybe she still has some pain from her injuries.

Grammar Check

関係詞

1. 関係代名詞：接続詞＋代名詞の働き

    Joshua is the engineer who invented this small engine. <主格>
    (ジョシュアがこの小型エンジンを開発した技術者です)
    I have a friend whose father is a famous scientist. <所有格>（父親が有名な科学者である友だちがいます）
    Isabella works for a company that has its headquarters in Seattle. <目的格>
    (イザベラはシアトルに本社がある会社で働いています)
    We went to the seaside on the weekend, which was really relaxing. <非制限用法>
    (私たちは週末に海岸へ行きました。それは本当にくつろげました)

	主格	所有格	目的格
先行詞が人	who / that	whose	whom [who / that]
先行詞が人以外	which / that	whose	which / that

2. 関係副詞：接続詞＋副詞の働き（＝前置詞＋関係代名詞）

    I remember the day when I met Kitty for the first time. <時>（キティに初めて会った日を覚えています）
    This is the TV station where Claire works. <場所>（これはクレアが働いているテレビ放送局です）
    That is why Joan comes to the conference every year. <理由>（それはジョアンが毎年会議に出る理由です）
    This is how I designed the machine. <方法>（こうやって機械を設計しました）

Unit 15 Did You Watch TV Last Night? *subjunctives*

Warm-up

Listen and fill in the blanks with the words. Then choose the statement (A) or (B) that describes what you see in the picture.

(A) The man wearing a tie is using a (   ).

(B) The man with short hair is holding a (   ) in his right hand.

Answer (   )

1 Reading

Read the passage below and then do the exercises that follow.

Did you happen to watch that documentary on Channel 4 last night? You didn't? Oh, too bad. It was great. It was all about how rockets that launch communication satellites into space are designed and built. We got to see who the world's most important rocket manufacturers are, and got a good look inside a rocket engine, and learned why the
5 engines are so powerful. The documentary even broke down rocket-building finances for us. They concluded that if you try to reduce your costs too much and, at the same time, try to speed up your production time, you will be in big trouble. You will fail, in other words. Makes sense, doesn't it?

One rocket engineer, a man named Ted Bryson who, believe it or not, is from right
10 here in Northfield, put it like this: "If you believe what everyone says, it seems that we at BEC are doing everything right. We think of the engine's function first and foremost, not what it costs to build it. A small group of engineering companies are in the process of developing an economical, standard-design rocket. If they can cooperate with other companies like ours, they will no doubt succeed. And if they are successful, they will
15 corner the European market for mid-sized rockets for years to come."

Anyway, while I was watching the documentary—they were showing an international conference on rocket production being held somewhere—I noticed a young woman walk in front of the camera carrying a large briefcase. She had long black hair, and was quite pretty, and she appeared to walk with a slight limp. She looked really familiar. It might
20 have been on TV that I saw her. Or maybe she rode in my taxi. I can't stop thinking about her, though. But I am sure that I've seen her before. I wonder where? You might say it's a kind of mystery.

Notes **communication satellites**「通信衛星」　　**break down**「分析する」　　**first and foremost**「真っ先に」　　**in the process of**「〜の過程で」　　**standard-design**「標準設計の」　　**cooperate with**「〜と提携する」　　**no doubt**「必ず」　　**corner**「独占する」　　**with a slight limp**「少し足を引きずって」　　**look familiar**「見覚えがある」

Exercises

A Vocabulary

Match the words on the left below with their meanings (a-e) on the right. Write the letters of each meaning on the lines.

1. documentary _____
2. function _____
3. conclude _____
4. finances _____
5. economical _____

a. a thing's main use; purpose
b. money available to a business or person
c. non-fiction TV programme or movie
d. reasonably priced; cheap
e. to accept something as true; to decide

B True or False

Choose the word in bold that correctly completes each sentence. Then, based on the information in the reading passage, circle T if the sentence is true or F if it is false.

1. The BEC system of engineering seems to be the (**good** / **best**) way.　　T F
2. The private group of companies (**are** / **is**) likely to become very successful.　　T F
3. The TV reporters spent some time (**interviewed** / **interviewing**) the young woman.　　T F

C Choosing

Choose the correct answer (A) or (B) for each question below.

1. What did Channel 4 broadcast last night?
   (A) A news program about the Northfield case
   (B) A documentary about rocket design and manufacture

2. What most likely will be the outcome of the group of companies' cooperative efforts?
   (A) They will end up in big trouble and perhaps even fail.
   (B) They could dominate the European market for medium-sized rockets for years to come.

3. Who was the young woman who walked in front of the camera?
   (A) Perhaps it was the same Sonia who disappeared from the hospital.
   (B) She was probably just one of Channel 4's camera operators.

2 Conversation

A Q&A

Listen to the conversation with three speakers and see the graphic. Then listen to each question and fill in the blanks, and choose the best answer.

Today's Sales Share of Rocket Parts

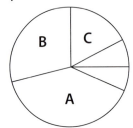

1. Can _____ _____ the new design?
   (A) The design will make the parts much stronger.
   (B) The pipes will slope outward much more steeply.
   (C) The joints will be much more difficult to make.

2. Look at the pie chart. Which position represents BEC's _____ _____?
   (A) Position A   (B) Position B   (C) Position C

3. What is the _____ _____ the new design for BEC?
   (A) It will increase its sales staff.
   (B) It will become the second largest manufacturer in the country.
   (C) It will be taken over by a larger parts manufacturer.

B L&F

Now, as you listen to the conversation again, fill in the blanks.

reporter: Mr Bryson. We listened carefully to your presentation, and I am sure we were all excited to hear about your new ideas. For our viewers, can you simply ₁( ) your talk?

Ted: Well, to make a good high-pressure joint, the engineers usually make the pipe end slope outwards a little bit. However, we have ₂( ) that by using a rounder pipe end.

reporter: What does that mean for engine designs?

Ted: It makes the parts easier to make and a lot ₃( ). Judging from today's sales data, we are the third. But if things continue as they are now, we will be the ₄( ) largest producer of rocket parts in the country.

reporter: Wow, that's fantastic. I ₅( ) you lots of luck in your business.

3 Text Completion

Select the best choice for each numbered blank in the text below.

Oh no, not again. This is the second time I've lost my car key. I know I had it this morning ------- I drove here. I parked in my regular place, but I can't remember what I did after that. What did I do? Well, I was in my office until ten. That's when the meeting started. What ------- somebody stole the key? I usually keep all my papers there. If it has been stolen, I ------- go to the police right away. -------
1.   2.   3.   4.

1. (A) as if
   (B) because
   (C) otherwise
   (D) without

2. (A) about
   (B) if
   (C) of
   (D) with

3. (A) need
   (B) ought
   (C) should
   (D) used

4. (A) Better yet, I'd ask my wife to bring me a spare key.
   (B) But I'll keep looking for my car all day.
   (C) The police couldn't care less.
   (D) But I can't go without my bike.

4 Writing

A Rewrite each sentence below according to the instructions.

1. Since we don't make economical engines, we can't corner the market. (仮定法過去に)

2. I didn't concentrate on the design, so I wasn't able to succeed in completing it.
   (仮定法過去完了に)

3. <u>If you didn't help me</u>, I couldn't have made a decent presentation.
   (下線部を Without で始めて)

B Rearrange the words in the parentheses to make correct sentences.

4. ケイトは軽傷であったけれど、1か月以上の間入院しています。

   Even though Kate's injuries were minor, she (for / been / has / in / the hospital) over one month.

5. その会社は通信衛星を宇宙に運ぶ革新的なロケットを製造しました。
   The company produced (an innovative / delivers / that / communication satellites / rocket) into space.

   _____

6. 他の企業と協力できれば、私たちは世界市場で成功するでしょう。
   If we can work with other companies, we (in / market / succeed / the global / will).

   _____

C Fill in the missing words to complete each sentence.

7. あまりにも急速にあまりにも多く体重を減らそうとすれば、健康を害することになります。
   If you try to (　　　　　) (　　　　　) too quickly and too much, it can harm your (　　　　　).

8. もっと注意深く答えを見直していたら、あなたはミスを減らせたでしょう。
   If you (　　　　　) reviewed your answers more (　　　　　), you would (　　　　　) eliminated your (　　　　　).

5 Look and Write

As you look at the illustration below, fill in the blanks in the paragraph that follows with words from the box. Change the word's form where necessary.

| come   crew   know   meet   walk   where |

This looks like either a big hotel or a train station. It is probably in Germany, ₁(　　　　　) a big international conference has just finished. The TV ₂(　　　　　) look pretty excited. Maybe some of their predictions about the engineering business have ₃(   ) true. Maybe they have ₄(   ) some of the top people in the field. What they haven't realised is that the person at the centre of a big news story is ₅(   ) past them right now. If they ₆(   ) that, what would they say?

Grammar Check

仮定法

1. 仮定法過去：現在の事実に反することの仮定

If ＋ S ＋過去形〜, S ＋ would (could, might, should) ＋動詞の原形〜

If I knew his email address, I would invite him to the party.
(もし彼のメールアドレスを知っていれば、パーティーに招待するでしょう)

If I got a pay rise, I would buy a new electric car.
(もし給料が上がれば、新しい電気自動車を買うでしょう)

2. 仮定法過去完了：過去の事実に反することの仮定

If ＋ S ＋ had ＋過去分詞〜, S ＋ would (could, might, should) ＋ have ＋過去分詞〜

If Thomas hadn't broken his leg, he could have become a professional footballer.
(もしトーマスが脚を折らなかったなら、プロのサッカー選手になれたでしょう)

Had Judy made a good presentation, she could have improved her company's reputation.
(もしジュディが良いプレゼンをしていたら、彼女の会社の評判を高めることができたでしょう)

3. 仮定法の慣用的表現

Without your advice, I **couldn't do** the work.
(もしあなたのアドバイスがなかったら、その仕事をすることができないでしょう)

If it had not been for the heavy snow, the plane **could have taken off**.
(もし大雪でなかったら、その飛行機は離陸できたでしょう)

Shirley behaves as if she were a little girl.
(シャーリーはまるで幼い少女のように振る舞います)

> 著作権法上、無断複写・複製は禁じられています。

Kickoff English Mystery		[B-876]
『キックオフ ミステリー』— 楽しく学べる総合英語		

| 1 刷 | 2019年 4月 1日 |
| 3 刷 | 2024年 4月 25日 |

著 者	テリー・オブライエン	Terry O'Brien
	三原　京	Kei Mihara
	宇佐美　彰規	Akinori Usami
	木村　博是	Hiroshi Kimura

発行者　南雲　一範　Kazunori Nagumo
発行所　株式会社　南雲堂
　　　　〒162-0801　東京都新宿区山吹町361
　　　　NAN'UN-DO Co., Ltd.
　　　　361 Yamabuki-cho, Shinjuku-ku, Tokyo 162-0801, Japan
　　　　振替口座 : 00160-0-46863
　　　　TEL: 03-3268-2311(営業部:学校関係)
　　　　　　　03-3268-2384(営業部:書店関係)
　　　　　　　03-3268-2387(編集部)
　　　　FAX: 03-3269-2486

編集者	加藤　敦
製　版	橋本　佳子
装　丁	Nスタジオ
検　印	省　略
コード	ISBN978-4-523-17876-7　C0082

Printed in Japan

E-mail　nanundo@post.email.ne.jp
URL　https://www.nanun-do.co.jp/